"Pastor Steven has written the best book I've ever read on overcoming the lies that hold us back. If you read this prayerfully and take the truths of *Crash the Chatterbox* to heart, God will help you win the battles in your mind and become the person He created you to be."

—CRAIG GROESCHEL, lead pastor, LifeChurch.tv, Edmond, OK; author of *Fight*

"Crafted around four powerful confessions, *Chatterbox* unearths, exposes, and refutes lies and half truths all of us are tempted to believe about ourselves. Steven's direct writing style will keep you engaged. His insights will make you think. But most important, these four confessions will free you to embrace the life God has called you to live."

—ANDY STANLEY, senior pastor, North Point Church, Alpharetta, GA; author of *Enemies of the Heart*

"I believe God's truth. I want to live God's truth. But sometimes I have a hard time hearing God's truth when negative inside chatter and self-doubt run like a ticker tape through my mind. Pastor Steven's vulnerability, biblical insights, and practical advice make *Crash the Chatterbox* a resource I will turn to again and again. This book can be a game changer for you."

—LYSA TERKEURST, *New York Times* best-selling author; president of Proverbs 31 Ministries

"Every one of us at some point deals with fears and self-doubt, with internal conflict about whether we are good enough or successful enough, or whether our past will forever haunt our future. Be inspired and encouraged as you discover what God really says about you in *Crash the Chatterbox*."

—BRIAN HOUSTON, senior pastor, Hillsong Church, Sydney, Australia

"On the pages of his brilliant new book, my friend Steven teaches us how to block out the toxic lies of the Enemy and instead let the truth of God become the soundtrack to our lives. Don't let all the chatter get the best of you. Read these pages, and be strengthened in Christ."

—MATT REDMAN, Grammy Award–winning songwriter and worship leader

"Steven Furtick unlocks powerful stratagems for silencing the inner critic that entangles the believer in a quagmire of self-doubt, fear, and unbelief. *Crash the Chatterbox* is a study in course correction with hard-won lessons for rediscovering, reenergizing, and reengaging your God-given dreams."

—T. D. JAKES, *New York Times* best-selling author; bishop of The Potter's House, Dallas, TX

"Steven Furtick's new book is an insightful and readable approach to the daily barrage of destructive thoughts we all experience. You will be encouraged and empowered as you discover what God thinks of you and how that affects every facet of your life."

—JUDAH SMITH, lead pastor, The City Church, Seattle, WA; *New York Times* best-selling author of *Jesus Is _____*.

"When we use our weaknesses to strengthen our faith, we turn our greatest liabilities into weapons in the hands of Christ. I love how my friend Steven Furtick humbly reveals his own struggles as he strives to crash the chatterbox in his life. Don't count yourself out just yet; your struggle is only the starting place of God's purpose in your life."

—MARK BATTERSON, lead pastor of National Community Church, Washington DC; *New York Times* best-selling author of *The Circle Maker*

"It's time to break out and fight back. Don't be held in bondage anymore. Let Steven Furtick help you crash the chatterbox and silence the voice of insecurity in your life. You were created for more. Now take your place in the center of God's calling."

—CHRISTINE CAINE, founder, A21 Campaign; best-selling author of *Undaunted*

"Often the most crippling negativity we hear comes from our own mind. In *Crash the Chatterbox*, Steven Furtick offers an effective antidote. In a refreshing and relatable style, he lays out the strategy to overcome the inner critic that hinders us from hearing the voice of God, receiving His glorious affirmation, and accomplishing His perfect will."

—ROD PARSLEY, World Harvest Church, Columbus OH; *New York Times* best-selling author of *Culturally Incorrect*

"What you're getting in *Crash the Chatterbox* is the reassuring and honest feedback from a great friend. It may not be what you wanted to hear, but it will definitely help you get where you're going."

    —PERRY NOBLE, senior pastor, NewSpring Church, Anderson, SC;
      author of *Unleash!*

"I love Steven Furtick's commitment to a purpose that is greater than his problems. In *Crash the Chatterbox,* Steven helps us see that our greatest barrier is the very bridge God uses to take us to our divine purpose."

    —KERRY SHOOK, founding pastor of Woodlands Church, Houston, TX;
      coauthor of the national bestsellers *One Month to Live* and *Love
      at Last Sight*

"The Enemy's greatest fear is that you'll discover who you really are, what you're really worth, and where you're headed. Steven Furtick amplifies the call of God in your life so that you can crash the chatterbox of the Enemy's lies and move forward with confidence in Christ."

    —JENTEZEN FRANKLIN, senior pastor, Free Chapel, Gainesville, GA;
      New York Times best-selling author of *Fasting*

"There are only a handful of Christian leaders in my generation who preach the Word of God with as much passion and conviction as Steven Furtick. In *Crash the Chatterbox* you will be encouraged by a committed man of God who is gifted at bringing God's truth to life. Through Steven's determination to follow God wholeheartedly, you will find the strength to chase after God's calling for you."

    —ISRAEL HOUGHTON, Grammy Award–winning songwriter
      and worship leader

"If you've ever felt the sting of a critic or the discouragement of that voice of doubt in your head, then you need to crash the chatterbox and renew your mind. This book will teach you how to shut out the noise and start living your purpose."

    —DR. JACK GRAHAM, pastor, Prestonwood Baptist Church, Plano, TX

"In a world where we are bombarded by countless voices that influence our every step, it's often difficult to discern the voice of truth. Pastor Steven Furtick shows us how to surgically cut through the chatter and hear the voice of God. This book is a must-read!"

—STOVALL WEEMS, lead pastor, Celebration Church, Jacksonville, FL;
author of *Awakening*

"I have rarely read a book with as much personal transparency and honesty as I found in this book by Steven Furtick. If you want to get out of your own way and move forward in God's plan, *Crash the Chatterbox* is for you."

—KEVIN GERALD, lead pastor, Champions Centre Church, Tacoma, WA

"In *Crash the Chatterbox,* Steven Furtick helps readers understand the volatile nature of listening to the wrong voices in our lives. And with humor, insight, and clarity, he reveals what it takes to open up the lines of communication with the only voice that truly matters—the voice of God."

—ED YOUNG, pastor, Fellowship Church, Dallas, TX;
author of *Sexperiment*

"I admire Steven Furtick's refusal to allow anything to push him off the path God has placed before him. In *Crash the Chatterbox* he lets us into the struggle that he's faced embracing his calling. His transparency and honesty will give you the courage to fight on."

—CLAYTON KING, president, Crossroads Ministries;
teaching pastor, NewSpring Church, Anderson, SC

"In *Crash the Chatterbox,* Steven Furtick gives us a how-to guide to actually apply the truth of how God feels about us so we can live empowered lives."

—BIL CORNELIUS, author of *Today Is the Day*; founding pastor,
Bay Area Fellowship, Corpus Christi, TX

"Steven Furtick's willingness to be vulnerable makes the truth he is relaying easy to digest. If you're tired of circling around the same struggles, you will find an accessible off-ramp to a freer life in *Crash the Chatterbox.*"

—JOHN BEVERE, cofounder of Messenger International;
author of *Relentless*

NEW YORK TIMES BEST-SELLING AUTHOR

STEVEN FURTICK

CRASH THE CHATTERBOX

HEARING GOD'S VOICE ABOVE ALL OTHERS

MULTNOMAH
BOOKS

CRASH THE CHATTERBOX
PUBLISHED BY MULTNOMAH BOOKS
12265 Oracle Boulevard, Suite 200
Colorado Springs, Colorado 80921

Details in some anecdotes and stories have been changed to protect the identities of the persons involved.

Hardcover ISBN 978-1-60142-456-3
eBook ISBN 978-1-60142-458-7

Cover design by Ryan Hollingsworth

Published in association with the literary agency of Fedd & Company, Inc., P.O. Box 341973, Austin,
TX 78734.

Published in the United States by WaterBrook Multnomah, an imprint of the Crown Publishing Group,
a division of Random House LLC, New York, a Penguin Random House Company.

MULTNOMAH and its mountain colophon are registered trademarks of Random House LLC.

The Cataloging-in-Publication Data is on file with the Library of Congress.

Printed in the United States of America
2014—First Edition

10 9 8 7 6 5 4 3 2 1

SPECIAL SALES
Most WaterBrook Multnomah books are available at special quantity discounts when purchased in bulk by
corporations, organizations, and special-interest groups. Custom imprinting or excerpting can also be done
to fit special needs. For information, please e-mail SpecialMarkets@WaterBrookMultnomah.com or call
1-800-603-7051.

For Holly

####

Every chatterboxer needs a Mickey and an Adrian.
You are both to me.

CONTENTS

SECTION 4. GOD SAYS I CAN

INTRODUCTION

Chatterboxing

I wish I had a little devil on my left shoulder. I could flick him off and tell him to go to hell. Then I could fist-bump the angel sitting on my right shoulder and get on with doing all the things God has called me to do.

That would change everything.

I'd discover an unshakable confidence. It wouldn't be borrowed from the ever-changing assessments of others. I would instinctively offer my weaknesses as a platform for God's power instead of typecasting myself as someone God couldn't use due to my endless character flaws.

I'd be unstoppable because the devil wouldn't be able to dominate my mind with the kinds of fears that control me a lot of the time. Then I would be able to move forward in faith without being scared of failure or rejection or the sacrifice required to obey God.

I'd never again be paralyzed by condemnation or bullied by feelings of unworthiness. And at the end of each day I'd go to sleep in perfect peace because I'd be finishing the day with no shame, no regrets, no need to sew any fig leaves to conceal anything.

I'd be nearly immune from discouragement, because I would stop wondering if the sky was falling every time I faced a new challenge. I'd see my biggest obstacles as my greatest opportunities...and all the other stuff you read on Starbucks cups.

Unfortunately, there's no devil on my shoulder.

What's worse, there's no angel either.

Instead, I've got this ceaseless war going on inside my heart and my head. I'm waging it every millisecond of every minute of every hour of every day—nights, holidays, and weekends too.

####

I wake up every day to the crow of the chatterbox.

Here's a transcript of my internal dialogue from a recent morning. It's a real-time example of the kind of chatter that can derail my day before it even gets started. Sometimes over the most ridiculous things you can imagine.

The thoughts are flying so fast now that I can't keep track, much less sort them out and put them where they belong. Thinking about these thoughts at all only seems to feed them. That's why they keep overpowering me, because I keep feeding them. I know this, but it never stops me from doing it. Not this time, not ten years ago, and it won't be any different ten years from now, I'm beginning to believe.

This is so stupid. I'm being so stupid.

It's only a light bulb.

A burned-out light bulb has turned into a mini-midmorning meltdown in my mind, and I can't find the switch to shut it off. The meltdown, I mean, not the light bulb.

So I'm standing in the shower, and the light bulb is out, and it's like the sky is falling.

As soon as I stepped into the shower, I noticed, for the third time, that the middle bulb was out over the sink on the other side of the bathroom. Now that I'm in the shower, stranded, phoneless, how am I going to put in Evernote that the light bulb is out? With my pathetic attention span, what are the chances I'll remember to replace the light bulb after I get out?

I definitely don't have time to change the light bulb—I'm already going to be ten minutes late for this meeting. If there's no traffic. I'm always running late for meetings. I'm a late person. It's because I hit the snooze button three times every morning, because I'm spiritually apathetic. Pastor Mickey used to get up at 5 a.m. and spend two hours with God, and he said, "He who runs from God in the morning will scarce find Him throughout the day." They should put that on a Starbucks cup too.

Either way, God is gone for the day, and it's not even 9 a.m. And now I'm running twelve minutes late, and the light bulb is still out.

I'm screwed.

And who am I kidding? Even if I had time to change the light bulb, yeah, right, like I have a clue where Holly keeps them. Now that's really pathetic. What would people think if they found out about that one: the woman changes all the light bulbs around that house! What kind of example am I setting for my kids?

Did I even pray with the kids last night? the night before that?

Dunno. But I did Instagram *that sunset shot with the kids at the creek last Friday. So there's that.*

"Cock-a-doodle-do." The chatterbox informs me that I'm *fourteen* minutes late…and I suck as a person.

I'm feeding the machine, and it's eating me alive.

And the chatter will continue to race through my mind until I decide to downshift and put things back in perspective: *Calm down, Furtick. It's. Just. A. Light bulb.*

Just like that, if only for a split second, the chatterbox gives way. And I get on with my day.

Unfortunately, it won't be long until the chatterbox sounds off again. Probably next time about something much more serious than a light bulb. So much doubt, panic, raw impulse, and bogus conjecture stream through my mind. My soul sometimes feels like a Twitter feed where I'm following a million of the most annoying people ever, and I can't find the Unfollow button.

But God is faithful to speak too. His voice rises from the pages of His Word, which is the exact expression of His will. He speaks, not only on Sunday mornings in the sanctuary where the congregation is gathered, but also in the stillness of His works scattered across the night skies. His Spirit speaks with promptings that are not audible—often they are much louder than that—always in perfect harmony with the Scriptures and always resounding with perfect wisdom.

And in every season of my life, God has sent reminders to confirm that He has perfectly designed me and totally enabled me for everything He's called me to do. Sometimes He'll do that through a simple picture, song, text, or conversation that rings with affirmation for days.

Other times, at critical junctures, God has spoken dramatic words of encouragement over my life.

A few years ago I was on a plane headed home, and I looked out the window during the descent. The sunset seemed to be painting the skyline in neon orange, illuminating the city where I had just moved to start a church. It was a glowing visual that set the scene for God to speak to my heart: *This is your city. I've called you here to pour out your life for My cause. Be confident, because everywhere you set your foot belongs to Me, and you belong to Me, and together we're going to take this city for My glory.*

I'm sure my translation of this conversation isn't word perfect, because you know how tricky cross-cultural communication with God can be. Plus, I can't find the notebook where I frantically scribbled every word of those impressions.

The part I'm sure of is that I heard God encouraging me at a time when I really needed it. We were only a couple of months into getting our new church off the ground. I needed some reassurance, and God delivered.

And it was His voice piercing through the roar of my doubts that lifted my perspective. It was just enough to keep me moving forward in faith.

Now I'd like to ask you a few questions.

Is it possible to be the kind of person who can be distracted to the point of utter despair by a blown light bulb and still hear God calling you to do great things as you stare down at your city through a sunset?

Can God's voice coexist with maniacal chatter—within the same person?

And how can I silence the voice of the enemy *when the enemy is in me*?

Can you relate to this contradiction?

I used to think that someone who struggled with the kinds of weaknesses I deal with daily was useless to God. I felt so often like I was drowning in internal dialogue I couldn't control. It had been the soundtrack of my life for as long as I could remember. I had hoped these problems would finally be fixed when I became a committed Christian. And I hoped for it again each time I experienced spiritual highs along the way in my journey of faith.

But the beat went on.

Yet everything changed when I began to realize *God has given us the ability to choose the dialogue we believe and respond to.* And once we learn how, we can switch from lies to truth as deliberately as we can choose the Beatles over Miley Cyrus on satellite radio.

Choosing to believe this, moment by moment, and acting on it is the most important habit you will ever develop.

It is the key to pressing ahead and doing God's will anyway, even as you are bombarded with thoughts, feelings, and even facts about why you can't do it.

Why you shouldn't do it. And why you'll never be able to do it. Why you're too dysfunctional, too petty, too immature, too melancholy, too impulsive…

I'm now awakening to the reality that we can access the power of God's promises to constantly crash the system of our broken beliefs. I'm learning how to overpower the shouts of the Enemy by bending my ear to the whisper of God's supernatural truths about my identity in Him and His strength in me. This isn't something I did once and now it's over or something I can afford to do occasionally when it's convenient. It requires constancy. It's the only way I know to be the father, husband, leader, friend, and believer that God says I already am, the kind of person I am straining to believe I can become.

Winning the war of words inside your soul means learning to defy your inner critic. But that's easier said than done. And I think many times, as believers, we sense we are losing this war. But we don't know what to do about it because we don't know where to find the weapons, and we wouldn't know where to aim them if we did.

In other words, we feel powerless to crash the chatterbox.

And now would probably be a good time to explain exactly what I mean by that.

1

Subverting the Sabotage

Beware of no man more than of yourself;
we carry our worst enemies within us.

—CHARLES SPURGEON

I'm losing myself, I'm stuck in the moment
I look in the mirror, my only opponent

—JAY-Z

The term *chatterbox* is my way of representing the lies we believe that keep us from accurately and actively hearing God's voice.

So how can we even begin to understand this invisible chatterbox?

It's quite complicated, as you can imagine. But we have to start somewhere.

Jesus said that when the devil lies, "he speaks his native language, for he is a liar and the father of lies."[1] However, as I said in the introduction, our most immediate problem isn't the devil on our shoulders but a deeper reality about the condition of our hearts and minds. To blame all our wrong thinking solely on the devil is to ignore obvious practical considerations, scientific facts, and most important, other clear biblical teachings.

Like this one: the apostle Paul talks with great openness about something that is at work within him, waging war against his mind and making him a prisoner.[2] Here's one of the greatest Christians who ever lived, talking about an enemy within that is terrorizing his freedom in Christ. And in doing so, he doesn't mention the devil. Rather, he talks about what's happening in his mind.

Because it's in the mind that the transmission of God's plans for our lives either succeeds or fails.

I read online that the average person has more than sixty thousand thoughts per day, and over 80 percent of these thoughts are negative. Is that accurate? I don't know. Honestly, the website seemed sketchy. And I'm no expert in the science of the subconscious. The other day I saw an R.E.M. anthology called *Part Lies, Part Heart, Part Truth, Part Garbage.* That pretty much sums up my understanding of the way the human mind works. And I don't want this to turn into a Wikipedia article about neuroscience.

But let's think together about the possibility that 80 percent of our thoughts are not only devoid of any power to help us but actively work against us. When we allow our thoughts to go unchecked, a steady drip of lies cements the wrong patterns within our minds, building a Berlin Wall of bad beliefs.

I wonder how much of its forty-eight-thousand-word quota your chatterbox has already filled today?

Did you hear it in the closet while you were getting dressed, telling you that it doesn't matter what you put on, that nothing will look good on you because you're too flabby, too bony, too pale, too old, or, in a single word, defective?

Did you hear it in the office where you work or in the home where you raise your children, telling you there's no point in trying so hard because no one ever notices anyway?

Do you hear it loudest at the end of the day, when the mistakes and regrets and missteps can bounce around the room unobstructed by progress or perspective?

You sounded really stupid when…

How will you ever recover from…

Why would anybody want to be around a person like you, who…

God must be awfully disappointed in the way you…

Sounds Like

There's a word to describe this kind of barrage. I came across it for the first time recently. I'll share it with you now—it can be our word of the day.

logorrhea 1. pathologically incoherent, repetitious speech. 2. incessant or compulsive talkativeness; wearisome volubility.

The best part about our new word? It's pronounced law-*guh*-REE-*uh*. I'll let you make your own "sounds like" association.

Seriously, could there be a more fitting term to describe the way the chatterbox spews lies and garbage in our minds? It's a voice that drones on and on, always intimidating, always insinuating.

The chatterbox wants to inundate us with logorrhea. To wear us out until we don't want to try or until we have no idea what to do or how to answer our growing list of doubts and deficiencies.

And it's not just what this chatter says that makes it dangerous.

It's what it keeps us from hearing.

Most people go through life thinking God never speaks to them when in fact He's always speaking. To everyone. Always directing. Sometimes warning. Sometimes affirming. But we hear so little of what He says because our consciousness of His voice is obscured by our mental static.

What guidance was God trying to give you today that you didn't hear because it was buried by negative noise?

What wisdom did God want to share about your future that you missed because the logorrhea was too loud in the background?

You see, when we learn how to crash the chatterbox—to overpower the Enemy's lies with God's truths—we're not simply learning to think more cheerful thoughts or adopt a more pleasant disposition or find our happy place or improve our lot in life. There's much more at stake than that.

Brennan Manning wrote a line that perfectly describes what happens when the chatter gets the best of us: "Great deeds remain undone and the possibility of growth into greatness of soul is aborted."[3]

Think with me about the two parts of this double-edged warning.

"Great deeds remain undone..."

When lies are not confronted, callings are not fulfilled.

I'm not going to give you the "Don't die with your music in you" speech (at least not this early on), but I do want to ask a few reflective questions as we get started.

- At this point in your life, what great deeds are in danger of remaining undone because of lies that were planted in your past or fears that are looming in your future?
- Is there a throb or an ache because of a sense of purpose in your heart that remains unfulfilled? What weeds are growing in the cracks of some of the God-inspired ideas you've abandoned?
- How many contributions that God created you to make for His glory are still wrapped in good intentions because they've been neutralized by spiritual hesitation?
- What great deeds that God wants to accomplish in your future are absolutely dependent on your decision to confront these lies right now?
- What desperate needs are crying out to be met all around you that God cannot meet through you unless you confront the lies and discover the courage to fulfill your calling?
- How are the people closest to you—your kids, parents, spouse, friends—suffering because of the lies you believe?

The saddest part is, we'll never know all the great deeds that remain undone as a result of the undetected and unchecked lies in our lives. Most of us die with our music still in us. (Now look what you've made me do.)

My previous book, *Greater,* issued a call to an understanding that God is ready and willing to achieve a kind of greatness through our lives that is beyond human reach. *Crash the Chatterbox* is about using that understanding to short-circuit the thoughts and patterns that the Enemy employs to disrupt the greatness God has initiated.

"...and the possibility of growth into greatness of soul is aborted"

God is the only person who can be simultaneously 100 percent task driven and 100 percent relationally focused. That means He is equally concerned about what He's doing in me and what He's doing through me. In fact, it's the work He does in me that prepares and empowers me for the work He desires to do through me.

Through Jesus, God has gone to the most extravagant lengths possible so that He might know you and make Himself progressively and vividly known to you. He wants to show you things about who He is and who you are that flesh and blood cannot reveal and that trials and tribulations cannot diminish. He longs to communicate with you in tones, pitches, and frequencies that this world is not wired for, to fill you with affirmation that your soul has been thirsting for.

The chatterbox is the part of you that jams these signals, often in a way that's hard to pinpoint.

In his book *The War of Art,* Steven Pressfield writes about overcoming the battles that block creativity. He gives a systematic breakdown of what he calls "the Resistance"—the force that prevents us from getting the things done we're meant to do. He describes the effects like this:

> We feel like hell. A low-grade misery pervades everything. We're bored, we're restless. We can't get no satisfaction. There's guilt but we can't put our finger on the source. We want to go back to bed; we want to get up and party. We feel unloved and unlovable. We're disgusted. We hate our lives. We hate ourselves.[4]

This may be an extreme description, but I'm sure you've felt this way, or close to it, before. We all have.

When our minds and hearts are being assaulted by the suggestions and lies of the Enemy, we often don't even know what's causing our funk or what's behind our frustration. We just know we're stuck in a cycle of spiritual self-sabotage.

Undetected Undertones

One day I was trying to make a mental list of the lies that were driving some of the dysfunction in my life. The exercise turned out to be much more complicated than I had anticipated. And I'll tell you one reason why: the thing that makes deception so effective is that you can't detect it.

The chatterbox doesn't preface its lies with an announcement: *Attention! The thought you're about to think is absolutely toxic, designed to lead you away from the good and perfect will of your loving heavenly Father.*

Instead, like a distortion pedal, the chatterbox manipulates the truth.

So it won't sound like this: *Perhaps you should take steps toward spending more focused time reading your Bible, because God has so many promises and truths He wants to reveal to you today.*

More likely it will sound like this: *If you really loved God, you'd spend more time reading your Bible, like people do who have their priorities in order.*

Both of these statements contain a seed of truth. The seed is *I'm not reading my Bible enough. I should read it more.* Yet the essential messages couldn't be more opposite.

Listen to the undertones of the second statement compared to the first.

The first statement is rooted in a spirit of affirmation: *God desires to speak to you.* And it is presented in the form of an invitation—to come into His presence and receive the good things He has to offer. It suggests a realistic course of action: you don't have to reinvent your life overnight—just make some *steps toward* your destination.

The second statement is rooted in the spirit of condemnation: *You don't really love God.* This is a gross exaggeration and misinterpretation of the motivations of your heart. And it's followed by an accusation: *Other people love God more than you do. You don't measure up; you never have, and you never will.*

Why do we let ourselves talk to ourselves this way? Maybe because the internal dialogue is happening much faster than our current level of training has enabled us to defend against. The Enemy has quick hands that land swift, accurate blows.

Also, sometimes perhaps we stand by passively, waiting for God to fix the issues that He's called us to fight in His strength. If we're going to overcome the thoughts that hold us back, first we have to give up the hope that they'll ever go away. Every second you spend wishing God would take away a struggle is a forfeited opportunity to overcome.

And even though the fight against chatter is guaranteed to be a grueling one, with no end in sight, you have to fight back. Your spiritual life depends on it.

Because the voice you believe will determine the future you experience.

Rhythm and Response

Now, when I start talking about voices like this, you might think I'm slipping into some pseudopsychoanalytical mode. But isn't this how the scriptural story begins—with conflicting voices? The rhythm of Creation is marked by call and response.

As we read in Genesis, it started with light:

- "God said, 'Let there be light.'" *Call.*
- "And there was light." *Response.*[5]

The very first chapter of the Bible establishes a cadence of communication that declares the creative potential of the voice of God. The illumination of everything we see started with something God *said.*

On the other extreme, an altogether different voice—the voice of the serpent in the garden—introduced temptation and sin into the world. A Puritan named Thomas Watson put it this way: "It was by the ear, by our first parents listening to the serpent, that we lost paradise; and it is by the ear, by hearing of the word, that we get to heaven."[6]

This juxtaposition of truth with lies is front and center throughout Scripture:

- God's voice speaks with precision and power, inviting us into a way of life that is truly life.
- Opposing voices seek to draw us out of His presence through seduction and deception.

The Enemy's goal is to lure us into accepting his lies and limitations at face value. When we do, our faith will only work in fits and starts. The lion's share of the good things that God has planned for us will remain out of reach. And the fruit we bear for God's glory will be minimal.

The prophet Isaiah issued an invitation that still stands today: "Hear, and your soul shall live."[7] That is the invitation I believe God is issuing to us in the pages ahead.

And I declare: the lies of the chatterbox are about to meet a fifteen-million megawatt surge of God's power. If that sounds a little violent for your taste, consider these words from the apostle Paul, who gave us permission to "demolish arguments and every pretension that sets itself up against the knowledge of God, and…take captive every thought to make it obedient to Christ."[8]

Because, thankfully, spiritual warfare isn't hand-to-hand combat. God has given us supernatural weapons that have "divine power to demolish strongholds."[9] We crash the chatterbox by launching a counterattack through which we leverage the advantage we have as God's children: heaven's perspective.

This doesn't mean the chatter will end.

It just means that we'll have something stronger—and louder—to override it every time it starts.

It may help to think about it this way.

Currently, as I write, I'm listening to a worship album by Hillsong United on my iPhone. It's a pretty mellow album, so it does the trick to help me concentrate. I'm listening through my noise-canceling headphones. They're a real gift from God, because my wife is just across the room, talking to three of our female church staff members. I don't know what they're talking about. Maybe a pressing leadership or motherhood issue, maybe *Downton Abbey,* or maybe how they can't wait to read my next book that I'm working on so hard over here. Most likely *Downton Abbey.*

The point is, I don't know. They're less than fifty feet away from me, and they're talking, talking, talking; yet it doesn't bother me a bit. Doesn't interrupt me. Doesn't hinder my progress, isn't breaking my flow.

As long as I keep my headphones on and turned up loud, they can chat away, employing their conversational gifts to the fullest, and I'm cool in my own world. I'm tuned in to something different.

I want to be careful here to avoid any comparison between my wife and the chatterbox. It's just an analogy. But in the pages that follow, I want to show you how to do this same thing—block out noise—on a spiritual level.

Quiet the Riot

This book is built on four confessions. They are meant to function like noise-canceling headphones for your mind, heart, and soul. These are truths about God and truths about you that come straight from God's Word. The term *confession* has many connotations, but literally it means "to say with" God. So by filling our spiritual ears with these four declarations of truth, we receive and respond to what God says about who He is and who we are in Him.

Each of the four confessions will target one of the main areas in which the Enemy uses chatter to corrupt our souls and weaken our faith. And with the Spirit's help, we'll blow the lies of the chatterbox to smithereens.

The confessions are life-giving, faith-increasing statements that are designed for you to repeat in your heart and mind, even rehearse out loud. You can play them from the time you wake up and the chatterbox starts blasting reveille until the chatterbox starts trying to sing you to sleep at night with lullabies and lies, replays and regrets.

They're not magical statements, but they produce miraculous results when actively applied.

You may want to take a moment to get familiar with these four confessions, because they'll shape the foundation of the book, and hopefully they'll become a foundational part of *you* by the time we're finished.

Confession 1: *God says I am.*
Overpowering the lies of the Enemy in your insecurities

Confession 2: *God says He will.*
Overpowering the lies of the Enemy in your fears

Confession 3: *God says He has.*
Overpowering the lies of the Enemy in your condemnation

Confession 4: *God says I can.*
Overpowering the lies of the Enemy in your discouragement

The changes these confessions will incite in our lives are revolutionary. Not because the confessions are fancy or brilliant, but simply because they are *powerful*. And they are *God's truths*. In His hands and with your cooperation, they are little sticks of dynamite that will turn skyscrapers of harmful thinking into piles of rubbish.

Knowledge without application won't do the job, though. So we won't dwell too long on mere facts or theories. Instead, we become liberated from lies as we actively embrace the ways God wants to reimagine and re-create our hearts. In the process we are joined with Him as He aligns our lives with these new realities.

So are you ready to reload your listening device? Let's ask God to clear the space we need so that in the pages that follow we can receive the truths we encounter at the deepest level possible.

The first truth is this: *When it comes to hearing God's voice, identity always comes before activity.*

And that's a spiritual secret the chatterbox was hoping you'd never discover.

THE VOICE YOU BELIEVE
WILL DETERMINE
THE FUTURE YOU EXPERIENCE.

#CRASHTHECHATTERBOX

SECTION 1

In which we overpower

the lies of insecurity

with the truth

God says I am.

2

Cancel the Audition

What is it you're looking for in this endless quest? Tranquillity. You think if only you can acquire *enough* worldly goods, *enough* recognition, *enough* eminence, you will be free, there'll be nothing more to worry about, and instead you become a bigger and bigger slave to how you think others are judging you.

—Tom Wolfe, *A Man in Full*

I got hooked on *The Voice* recently. It's a singing contest reality show with a twist. And to me, the twist is what makes it worth watching.

You know that in most TV singing competitions, how cool people look or how likable they are can play a bigger part than their actual singing ability in determining whether the judges put them through to the next round of the competition. Well, not on *The Voice*, because the judges can't see the contestants. In the blind audition round, the judges are seated in big red chairs with their backs facing the contestants. And if judges like what they hear after a contestant starts singing, they hit a big red button. The button makes their chairs turn around, and a big neon light at the bottom of the chairs comes on, declaring, I WANT YOU. That means the judge is picking the contestant, sight unseen, to be on his team. The quality of the voice was enough to get one of the top musical talents in the world to commit to be the person's coach. He or she will be on that team for the rest of the competition. But I don't usually watch the rest of the competition, because the blind audition round makes for the best TV.

It's intense to see somebody singing her heart out for a panel of judges who may or may not choose her and can't even see her.

Sometimes all four judges turn their chairs around. Then Usher and Blake Shelton and Adam Levine from Maroon 5 and Shakira all start arguing over who gets to be the coach. Next thing you know, there's a full-blown debate about who discovered Justin Bieber and whose hips are lying. It's so strange to see these musical giants fighting over who gets to work with this previously unknown aspiring artist.

But the craziest thing to see is the times when *no* chairs turn around. That's a downright depressing scene, man. *Nobody* is choosing this person. *No* lights are shining. The message is clear: Nobody wants you. You're going home, rejected. Back to singing "Unchained Melody" at your cousin's wedding in Buffalo.

I guess it hit me halfway through the first episode I watched: most of us go through our lives like these contestants go through those blind auditions. Waiting on someone to hit a button. Auditioning our hearts out for acceptance and approval.

And all these judges we've appointed are sitting in chairs we've furnished in our minds. We have to get them to turn around somehow. To do something or say something—to prove something to someone. The panel of judges may vary from person to person, but our driving motivation is the same: *we're trying to escape a self-inflicted prison of insecurity.* And we need these people to do something or say something that will get us out.

Obviously, we *do* need people around us who can affirm our gifts, lift our spirits, and build our courage. God uses others as part of His plan to satisfy our craving to belong and our need to be loved. For proof, see Eve.

But the chatterbox, doing what it does, takes a perfectly good desire and distorts it beyond recognition.

The Ultimate Insult

Maybe we have our parents in one chair. In some cases they're not even around anymore, or maybe we don't see them much. But accusations they made or affirmations they withheld can keep us in a state of perpetual insecurity.

Maybe somebody you work with or go to school with occupies another chair, and if that person would include you, compliment you, notice you—*Hit that button!*—you'd be in.

Somebody you dated once is in the next chair, and if you could just *succeed*, then you'd be singing "take a look at me now," and she'd rue the day she ever walked away from you. And you'd be *justified!* Vindicated!

And finally good enough.

What's sad and stupid about all this, of course, is that none of these people has a button to hit.

What's even sadder is, the One who is sitting in the only chair that really counts has already turned around. The only One who has the power to give us true approval has already offered it, freely and fully.

But too often we can't sense this approval from God. Why? Because conflicting messages from the chatterbox are constantly incoming, and we can't get it all sorted out clearly enough to tell the truth from the lies. Part of the reason for this has to do with our misunderstanding about the nature of insecurity.

For years I thought of insecurity as the opposite of pride. Like, cocky people struggle with pride, and on the other end of the spectrum, godly, humble people have to struggle with insecurity.

But insecurity is much more than an extreme lack of confidence.

In some ways insecurity is the ultimate insult to God. Because when we allow insecurity to override God's purpose in our lives, we're implying that He didn't quite get the job done when He put us together.

If that sounds like an overstatement, I want you to look at one of my favorite Old Testament passages and consider what it means to people like you and me and how it casts a new light on the insecurities in our lives.

Your Daily Dose of Doubt

Jeremiah was a prophet. I know Three Dog Night claimed he was something different, and you're probably tired of hearing people brag about the quality of his wine, but this is a different deal, you know.

Jeremiah the *prophet* was endued with the kind of resilience that is reserved for people who have to face unusual resistance. During a time of political upheaval, he was called by God to preach a searing message of repentance to the people of his hometown. His message was rejected throughout most of his ministry. He lived in isolation, suffered persecution, and saw, from an earthly perspective, little success in his lifetime.

Now that you know the basic context of Jeremiah's calling and career, I think you'll see the striking significance of the words God spoke to him in his teenage years, as his ministry was just beginning.

The Scriptures record Jeremiah's memory of the conversation:

The word of the LORD came to me, saying,

"Before I formed you in the womb I knew you,
before you were born I set you apart;
I appointed you as a prophet to the nations." (Jeremiah 1:4–5)

These words have meant so much to me throughout my own ministry. Not because I consider myself a prophet to the nations. Rather, because they reveal a general truth about not only *how* but *when* God's approval comes to me. It's a reality that has become an anchor for my sense of security. A reality I need to revisit constantly.

I was half joking to my friend the other day about how ironic it is that preachers sometimes tend to be the most insecure people on the planet. I think it's partially because we have to confidently declare truths to others that we often have a hard time believing ourselves. This creates quite the inner conflict. Because you're up there telling people how they don't need to live for the approval of others, but as you're preaching, you're looking for external signs of approval from the people you're preaching to. Then when you finish preaching, you check your social-media stream to see what others thought about your sermon— maybe to find that not many people are thinking about your sermon at all. Embarrassing to admit, but it's true. Insecurity is a powerful force.

Of course, it doesn't hit me only when I step on the platform to preach. It's a cycle of doubt I deal with daily. I see others who seem so great at stuff I struggle with. I am flooded with doubts about whether I have what it takes to do what God has called me to do.

In the light of scriptures like the one we just read, however, this way of thinking is unbiblical and nonsensical on every possible level.

Before and Ever After

God told Jeremiah that He knew him and had handpicked him for his task. But God had made His choice not *after* Jeremiah proved his potential as a preacher or *after* Jeremiah demonstrated significant levels of consistency or proficiency. God chose Jeremiah *before* he was ever *born*. Before Jeremiah could do anything to merit God's acceptance, He hit the big button.

Perhaps the light of heaven shone a little brighter over Anathoth, the small town where Jeremiah was born and raised, when God made this announcement, signifying that He had spoken the first and final word concerning the destiny of this boy: *I want him. That one. Jeremiah. He's a good friend of Mine.*

So while Jeremiah would live to know great rejection from those he would minister to, he would never have to know what it was to be rejected by the God in whose Name he ministered. In obscurity as well as in public humiliation, he could know he was called and completely known by the One who knows all things. Not because of something good Jeremiah had done, and not to be undone by something bad Jeremiah might do at a later time.

God turned His chair around and hand selected Jeremiah to be a part of His plan before Jeremiah preached a single syllable of his first sermon.

I believe God wants to enlighten your life with this very same revelation, in this very moment. You don't have to sing a single note to get God—or anyone else—to notice you. Because before you ever breathed, before you even had the opportunity to show off or screw up, God declared,

I want you.
You're Mine. I've chosen you.
You belong. To Me.
And you can know that you always will, because you always have.
Before you were ever born, I knew you.

Put it this way: God has issued an announcement from His throne in heaven, and He wants you to know, *The audition has been canceled.*

He has not chosen you blindly but intentionally, even while knowing you inwardly and intimately. And let me tell you why this is some of the best news in the history of the universe: If this God has chosen you while totally knowing even the worst parts of you, then you no longer have to live *up* to anything. Instead, you are now empowered to live *out* of an awareness of divine acceptance.

This is the antidote to insecurity.

It means you already have the part. Now you are invited to play it with assurance. It's probably not the part of prophet to the nations. Most of us are called to live out our callings as dads, moms, husbands, and wives. As friends, neighbors, students, and teachers. As men and women moving through marketplaces, serving in churches, contributing in our communities, and, most of all, growing in our relationship with God.

But mark this: the nature of your calling does not indicate the level of God's approval of you. And the fact that others have gifts and opportunities you don't have doesn't diminish the intensity of God's intentionality about the things He created you to do.

Now, the chatterbox will not alert you to any of this. In fact, it will insist on the opposite.

Pushing More Buttons

Insecurity is insidious. So it cloaks itself in the guise of comparison. Nothing can kill contentment and feed insecurity like comparison. And now, more than any other time in history, we live in a culture of incessant comparison.

I was trying to post something on Instagram the other day, and it turned into the perfect illustration of my own insecurity. I had been studying for my sermon, and I wanted to share a picture of the process. But the books in the background of the first picture I took didn't look impressive enough.

Suddenly I became obsessed with positioning the picture just right—to show how studious I was. I must have spent ten minutes stacking and restacking the books around my desk. I knew it was getting out of control when I started pulling books off my bookshelf that I hadn't been using to prep for my sermon—and that I hadn't used in years—so they could be part of the picture. These were big theology books that had nothing to do with my subject, but it's hard to beat a twelve-hundred-page lexicon when you're trying to show the world what an intelligent preacher you are! It was silly and a little sad how much I felt the need to construct a certain image to present online. For what benefit? More Likes on Instagram. More button pushing.

I had to laugh to keep from being disgusted with myself. And, for the record, I deleted the picture. Then I got up and put the boring books back on the shelf.

This is a small, isolated example of the kind of insecurity that shows up every day. We have instant access to the lives of those we know, those we don't, those we can't stand, those we wish we were, those we'd give anything to measure up to.

Well, we don't exactly have access to their lives. We have access to the parts of their lives they'd like us to see. Nobody posts the shot of Tommy karate chopping his little brother in the sternum or Mandy rolling her eyes at her mom and slamming the door because she's not allowed to go to the movies at nine o'clock. Instead, people post the shot of Tommy holding the game ball or Mandy accepting the dance competition trophy. And the chatterbox uses all of this—the images we see of who we *think* others are and what we think they're doing—to make us feel we're boring by comparison. Even worthless.

This is one of the main reasons we struggle with insecurity: we're comparing our behind-the-scenes with everybody else's highlight reel.

We know all too well the stuff in our lives that should disqualify us from God's love and keep us from fulfilling His purpose. We know that we're disorganized, irritable, and easily distracted. We internalize our defects and infer that we're the only ones who struggle with these things.

But remember: every weakness you know about yourself, God knows in greater detail than you could ever imagine. He knows the defect as well as what *causes* the defect.

But God says you are something different from your defects—something far more than your flaws.

Before you were born—before any of your defects were apparent to you—they were absolutely apparent to God. That didn't stop Him from calling your name and setting you apart. He placed you on the earth at a certain time for a pre-decided purpose.

And even when you can't seem to get your act together, your identity is secure and completely intact. Because in Christ, who you are matters infinitely more than anything you do or cannot do.

Baptized and Beloved

Matthew's gospel provides a beautiful picture of this reality. As you read it, look for the similarities between this account and God's calling of Jeremiah.

As soon as Jesus was baptized, he went up out of the water. At that moment heaven was opened, and he saw the Spirit of God descending like a dove and alighting on him. And a voice from heaven said, "This is my Son, whom I love; with him I am well pleased." (Matthew 3:16–17)

Jesus had infinite power and potential. He personally embodied the most important calling and mission in history. He did so much in His lifetime that John would later say the world could not contain the books describing His works. Yet notice *when* He received His Father's approval: at the *beginning* of His ministry—before He even officially started His mission. Now, if the Father's acceptance of Jesus was based in something that preceded His accomplishments, what makes you think you could do anything to knock God's socks off or to obtain His acceptance through your accomplishments?

What makes you think you have to turn your life around before you can completely commit your life to God? What makes you think you have to impress God with your obedience before He will impart His grace to you? What makes you think you have to do things to get God to like you, much less love you? What makes you think you have to be the perfect spouse or parent before God will perfectly love you?

Many Christians spend a lifetime trying to achieve something that Jesus already achieved for them. God's acceptance isn't based on performance. It wasn't for Jesus. And because of what He did for you, it isn't for you either.

The acceptance He had, you have. The love He unconditionally received, you unconditionally receive.

Yes, Jesus was the Son of God. But through Him, you are a child of God with the same privileges.[1] That includes the privilege of having God look at you and say, "I am well pleased."

I Know He Is, but What Am I?

One of the most powerful confessions you can ever learn to make starts like this: "God says I am _____." Then get busy learning how to fill in the blank. The Bible is full of vivid descriptions of the kinds of labels you *should* wear as God's child.

Once you've made the decision to build your assessment of yourself exclusively on God's Word, the chatterbox loses its ability to trash-talk you into submission. And the more adept you become at talking smack *back* to the chatterbox, the more ingrained the reality of who you are will become.

Crashing the chatterbox is about learning to say things like this—out loud—daily.

God says...
...I am His masterpiece.
...I am His workmanship.
...I am established.
...I am sealed with His promise.
...I am redeemed.[2]

These five are just to get you started. We could fill the rest of the pages of this book with these kinds of statements—all made by God Himself about who He made us to be—that He desires for us to accept and *to believe.*

Here's the problem, though. You're likely to find it a whole lot easier to believe the things God says about Himself than the things He says about you. Have you noticed this?

For example, in John 8:12, Jesus makes a bold statement about Himself: "I am the light of the world." As bold as that statement is, followers of Christ accept it at face value. Of course He's the light of the world. He's *Jesus,* you know.

But guess what? The same Jesus who called Himself the light of the world had this to say about His followers: "*You are* the light of the world."[3]

Now, this I struggle with. There's a lot of darkness in me. A lot of ignorance and a lot of impurity. The chatterbox reminds me of this frequently.

I believe God is holy and blameless. But when He calls *me* holy and blameless, I figure He must have me confused with somebody else. Yet He means exactly what He says. And the more I rehearse what He says about me, the more my activity will align with my true identity, the more I will become what God has already said I am.

I saw a commercial the other day. I think it was for AT&T. It showed people using their products in all kinds of different settings, and it ended with a great tag line: "It's what you do with what we do." In other words, we can manufacture the goods, but the way you put them to use determines their usefulness.

That's what I'm trying to get across. God has created you, has given His Son for you, has sent His Spirit to live inside you—that's what He's done. He works miracles, He restores broken people, He uses the least likely and gives strength to the weak. He speaks truth over your life that is living and active. That's what *He* does. But it's what we do with what He does that determines our destiny.

So I confirm God's calling on my life when I learn to affirm my identity in Him. And I activate my identity when I refuse lies and walk according to specific redemptive truth.

- I don't like myself very much in this moment, but *I am loved.*
- I don't seem to be gaining much ground in this battle, but *I am more than a conqueror.*
- I don't have a lot of confidence in myself right now, but *I am strong and courageous.*
- I don't know how to fix this part of my life, but *I am healed and whole.*
- I don't know how long I'll continue to struggle with this sin, but *I am forgiven and free.*

How do I know?

Because *God says I am.*[4]

This confession—"God says I am…"—is the primary force that begins to reshape our paradigms by informing our identities as new creations.

Obviously, repeating these mantras every day, in and of itself, won't make you a better Christian or guarantee your spiritual success. Repeating positive confessions by rote simply makes you more like Stuart Smalley, not more like Jesus. And just because God chose you before you were born doesn't mean you can live like hell, take your devotion to Christ lightly, and still expect God's perfect will to be done in your life. Scripture and history are full of cautionary tales of people who, tragically, did not complete their assignments. God had much more in store for them than they ever experienced, because they stopped short in disobedience.

But this is the starting point, or—more likely—the starting-*over* point. You can't go any further until you realize that the worth of your activity for Christ cannot rise above your understanding of your identity in Him. And there is unlimited power in the Word of God. Power to overcome the warped ways we see ourselves. And power to reassemble the image of God that we haven't always reflected but have already received.

God spoke to my heart recently in a season when insecurity was getting the best of me. Here's the essence of what I felt like He said: *You're spending too much energy assessing other people's assessment of you. I want you to reinvest that energy into aligning your life with My acceptance of you.*

This was a breakthrough moment of clarity for me.

Accepting God's acceptance of me doesn't mean I'm going to stop trying. It means I'm going to stop *trying out.* And I am intentionally redirecting my obsession.

When the neurotic nag of insecurity gives way to a passionate discovery of the promises of God, the peace that follows is supernatural.

The chatterbox cannot control the thoughts and trajectory of the child of God who faces each day with this attitude: *I have nothing to prove, because I am already approved.*

Box Score

When my son Elijah started playing T-ball a few years ago, he didn't care much about the actual sport of baseball. But he was ecstatic about the opportunity to compete. One of the traits my older boy inherited from me is an irrational, unbalanced, borderline psychotic, insatiable passion for competition.

So imagine his chagrin (and my slight trace of paternal disappointment) when they explained that they don't keep score in T-ball. This, to me, is a harrowing and scandalous development in modern culture. You might say it is an affront to the game of T-ball I grew up loving on the Moncks Corner, South Carolina, rec fields. A game where there were winners and losers. Not winners and pretend winners. What a sham!

Well, as you might expect, my five-year-old shared my disillusionment. On the way home from the first game (which according to my unofficial score, we, the Mudcats, won *convincingly*), Elijah asked, "Daddy, if they don't keep score, how do I know if I win?"

It was a reasonable question. He had been frustrated throughout the game because he didn't really even understand the rules yet. And his batting skills left a lot to be desired. As did his fielding skills. And his basic hand-eye coordination. And general attention span.

But the biggest question, clearly, was this: Without a final score to consult, what's the point?

How will I know if I'm doing well?

I realized in that moment, as I looked at him in the rearview mirror of my Maxima, that we were going to have to make up our own system for keeping score. Just between me and my boy.

I explained the new plan to him. "Elijah, from now on I'm going to always be where you can see me, whether you're on the field or at bat, whatever. And anytime you do something—catch the ball, miss the ball, hit the ball, swing at the ball seven times and knock the tee over, get on base, don't get on base, dig a rock out of the dirt while you're waiting in left field and throw it at the center fielder—look at me. You'll know where to find me. And if I give you the thumbs-up, that's the sign you did a good job. That means you're winning. And when I give you the thumbs-up, give me thumbs-up back."

This system was the highlight of the season for me. And I think it was for him as well. It reduced the whole game to one ambition, one goal—the thumbs-up—from one person, his father.

All these people around. All these rules he doesn't understand. All these kids who are bigger, better, faster, and probably jacked up on hGH.

Isn't this a microcosm of how our lives feel sometimes? I don't completely understand the rules, and I'm surrounded by others who are smarter. Fitter. Funnier. Better.

But when we narrow our focus and know where to look for the approval of our Father, life takes on a glorious simplicity.

The burning question is no longer "What did *they* think of that?" Or even "What did *I* think of that?"

Now it's only "God, were You good with that? Thumbs-up? If You're good, I'm good."

His acceptance becomes my guidance. And my reward.

In the spirit of full disclosure, you should know that I may have bribed Elijah before every T-ball game with bonus video-game time to ensure that the thumbs-up was sufficient motivation to discourage rock throwing, temper tantrums, and meltdowns.

Therefore, Elijah's motivation was completely different from that of the rest of the team. He was coming from a place of childlike confidence: *It doesn't matter what the other kids think. Doesn't matter what the other parents think. Doesn't even matter what the coach thinks, really, because my father holds the reward. And whether I catch the ball or miss it, if I look over and see a thumbs-up from Dad, I'm playing Mario Kart tonight.*

When you realize that God is the only One who really has any lasting reward to give, He becomes the only One whose approval you desperately need. You can rest in the fact that you have it—in full measure—because the work of God's perfect Son, Jesus, secured your acceptance the moment you placed your faith in Him.

Before you ever win or lose, God has turned His face toward you. He has chosen you. And He is pleased.

I have a digital picture frame in my office, and I smile like an orangutan every time a certain picture comes across the screen. It's a five-year-old standing on first base in a Mudcats jersey with a smirk on his face, stretching his thumb toward a designated spot behind the first base line...

Probably thinking about Mario Kart.

ONE OF THE MAIN REASONS
WE STRUGGLE WITH INSECURITY:
WE'RE COMPARING OUR
BEHIND-THE-SCENES
WITH EVERYBODY ELSE'S
HIGHLIGHT REEL.

#CRASHTHECHATTERBOX

3

God Likes Me Too

Most of us were taught that God would love us if and when we change. In fact, God loves you so that you can change. What empowers change, what makes you desirous of change, is the experience of love. It is that inherent experience of love that becomes the engine of change.

—RICHARD ROHR

When I was in first grade, my mom sent me to school every day with a dollar for lunch money. She would send it in this little change purse, and don't you dare act like you never carried one. A step below the fanny pack, this particular rubber change purse was yellow and imprinted with a black smiley face on the front. Beneath the smiley face, a simple message: "Smile, God Loves You."

I'm sure the inspirational message was the reason my mom (God love her) selected that change purse over all the other ones. Or maybe it was on sale at Big Lots.

Either way, isn't it funny how vividly I remember that change purse and its message? "Smile, God Loves You." It's twenty-six years later, I'm a grown man with a first grader of my own, and I can still describe it in detail.

Obviously, I'm not the first person to remember something random from his childhood. But it's not just the object I remember. I can still recall how I *felt* seeing the smiley face reminding me every day to smile because God loves me. It made me feel happy. I believed what it said. I thought it was the coolest thing. I didn't know at that point in my life that this was not only a biblical sentiment but also a Christian cliché that had spawned a mini-industry. At that point I thought of it as a personal message just to me. Also, I didn't know that carrying a yellow smiley-face change purse much past the first grade would get you made fun of by Harry Walker, which would be the end of the yellow change purse.

Beyond all this, I had no idea at the time how hard it would be to maintain my first-grade sense of confidence in God's love throughout my teenage years, much less through my adult life. First-grade me understood innately what grown-up, screwed-up me strains to believe: God loves *me*.

I do get it on one level. God loves me. Yeah, yeah, because He *has* to. Because I prayed and asked Jesus to be my Savior. I did the deal. And God promised that anyone who would believe would be saved. Consequently, God loves me.

What I struggle with is believing that God loves me, not just because He has to, but also because He *wants* to. His love sometimes seems more like a universally accessible one-size-fits-all commodity than a personal expression of His desire to have a relationship with me. I just happened to get in on the group policy.

I wonder if you've ever used this other classic Christian cliché when dealing with someone who gets on your last nerve: "The Bible says I have to love everybody, but it doesn't say I have to like everybody."

I've said this, or something like it, on many occasions. There's a lot of truth in it. It's a way of acknowledging that, while believers have clear biblical obligations to be good to others, we can't always be expected to *feel* good about them. We can love them without liking them.

It's like a love loophole.

That's the way the chatterbox wants you to feel about the way God feels about you.

Tainted Love

The message of God's love for us is visibly and tangibly pronounced in all of creation and in God's involvement in every detail of our lives. So if the Enemy can't *conceal* that message, he'll do his best to *corrupt* it: *Sure, God loves you. Jesus died for you, just like He died for everyone else. That doesn't make you special. And it certainly doesn't mean He has to like you. Come on, you will admit, you're pretty hard to like. You don't even much like yourself. How could God like you?*

As strange as this sounds, many of us need to graduate to a first-grade understanding of the love of God. In the last chapter we saw how God accepts us unconditionally, based on our faith in His Son, not on any works we've accomplished. But the problem with a word like *acceptance* is that it can carry a connotation of tolerance. It doesn't necessarily communicate delight. Sometimes we use the word *acceptance* to describe a reluctant resolution: "Well, I don't like it, but I guess I'm just gonna have to *accept* it."

And here goes the chatterbox, cranking away again. Even something as beautiful and transformative as the love and acceptance of God can be taken out of context.

The Enemy can't downgrade the truth of love and acceptance that God has spoken over you. So, instead, he'll do everything in his power to misrepresent the tone of God's voice. That way, while you might believe that God's Word has declared forgiveness and redemption over your life, you silently feel as if God is giving it begrudgingly: *Oh, all right. I'll forgive you again. I'll help you again. I'll answer your prayer this time. But it doesn't mean I'm gonna like it.*

Why do we interpret God's motives this way? Or, as one of my friends likes to put it, why are we so *suspicious* of God's love for us?

One culprit that contributes to this type of chatterboxing is the whacked-out, though often well-intentioned, religious teaching many of us have encountered. When I first became serious about God, I frequently heard church people talk about how careful we must be that sin doesn't "break our fellowship with the Lord."

This terrified me. As a teenager, all I could think about was how, on Friday, when the cheerleaders wore their uniforms to school, I was going to end up looking lustfully at one of them, and—*crack!*—my fellowship with the Lord would be broken! I thought, *He won't be able to stand to look at me until Sunday, when I can get back to church. I'll borrow a paisley tie from my dad and get him to tie it so I can wear it, and I'll iron my khakis the night before or beg my mom to. I'll show up early for Miss Jo's Sunday school class and read the entire lesson ahead of time.*

Then maybe God will like me again. Perhaps then our fellowship will be unbroken or at least only slightly fractured.

It was exhausting trying to rightly relate to a God I saw this way.

Read It Right

I have a friend who works for a leader who is known for being remarkably driven and unusually intense. I asked my friend, "Isn't it hard to work for someone so demanding? How do you deal with it?"

I've never forgotten his answer.

He said, "Well, I used to have a tough time with it for sure and still do sometimes. But we had one conversation that changed everything for me. See, most of our communication happens by e-mail. And one time after he had sent me a few e-mails in a row telling me things I needed to fix and things I needed to work on, I just couldn't take it anymore. I went to him and said, 'I don't feel like I can do anything right, man. I don't feel like you like me. I feel like a failure.'

"And that's when he explained to me, 'The problem is, you're not reading my e-mails right. You're misrepresenting my *tone* in your mind. Of course I believe in you. Of course I like you. If I didn't, you wouldn't have a job. E-mails are tricky. You can't see my face when you're reading an e-mail. So here's what I want you to do. From now on I want you to read any e-mail I send you like I was smiling when I sent it. 'Cause that's the way I feel about you.'"

I wonder how much our lives would change if we started reading God's Word like He was smiling when He wrote it?

Of course the One who created us believes in us. Of course He likes us. Why else would we be here? Yes, there are things He is working on in us. Yes, our sin is serious and needs to be addressed head-on. No, God is not satisfied to leave us like we are, and sometimes this involves direct confrontation. There are some tough, almost unbearably stark statements in Scripture calling us to repent, to return, and to walk in the ways of God. There are warnings and consequences explained in no uncertain terms. The Bible isn't a book of butterfly kisses and sweet nothings.

But even God's correction is meant to convince us of His love.[1] Contrary to the condemnation and accusations of the chatterbox, which we'll dismantle more thoroughly in Section 3, even when God calls us out on something we're doing wrong, His purpose is to raise us up. Never to beat us down.

Everything changes the day you realize that not only does God love you but He actually likes you too. Not just because He has to. But because He wants to.

The God who made you is constantly smiling over you, and that ought to make you smile like a first grader opening his change purse on grilled cheese day. Furthermore, it ought to empower your perspective in every battle you face. How can you lose when a God who feels this way about you is fighting for you?

Broken and Hopeful

There's a song we sing a lot in our church right now, and it's incredibly powerful. The part I especially love says,

> The One who reigns forever
> He is a friend of mine.

You can feel tidal waves of confidence swelling within people when we sing that part.

Why does it resonate so much? It's not that people have never heard or declared that God is the One who reigns forever. Neither is it news to most Christians that we have a friend in Jesus. I believe it's the connection of those two colossal ideas that rocks us.

When we link a biblical understanding of God's authority with our personal experience of His intimacy, it melts down the mainframe of the chatterbox.

And that's exactly what we need, because most of us feel powerless when assaulted by feelings of inadequacy and insecurity. John 10:10 says that the thief comes "to steal and kill and destroy" the life that Jesus died to impart. And since the Enemy doesn't have the power to snuff out our lives literally, he works from within to steal our sense of victory. Think about it: the chatterbox can't keep you from winning, because the battle you're fighting was never yours to win. Therefore, you can't lose. The Enemy can't keep you from being who God says you are. But he *can* blind you from *realizing* who God says you are.

If he can't keep you from winning, he will do everything in his power to keep you from walking in full awareness of your victory.

That's why the collision of the confession of *who God is* (the One who reigns forever!) and the confession of *who I am in Him* (He is a friend of *mine*!) registers so effectively in our souls.

As we were singing that song in church recently, I turned around as unobtrusively as I possibly could from the front row and studied the faces of a few of the people who were singing it. Some of them I knew nothing about, but the expressions on their faces or the tears in their eyes gave me a few hints about their stories. I let my imagination fill in the blanks. I often do that during worship before I preach. I imagine what the people we're ministering to might be going through. It helps me connect more personally with the urgency of the truth we're presenting.

On this particular day I saw one woman, probably in her twenties, who wasn't lifting her hands or singing, like so many people around her were. But she didn't look angry. I'd say she looked equal parts broken and hopeful as she scanned the people around her. The emotional and tearful expression on her face seemed to say, *Is this really true? I hope it's true. These people sure seem to believe it. Is this God really a friend of* mine?

I wondered about the heaviness of accusation she might have carried with her into church that morning. What did she know too well about herself—perhaps a hidden part of her past or a present struggle no one else knew about—that made it difficult for her to sing out the words that were obviously touching her heart? (Maybe she just didn't like to sing. I understand that's a possibility, but I like my version better.)

Two rows past the young lady was someone I knew more about. He was also crying, which was unusual for his temperament but made sense, given his situation. This man (I'll call him Bill) has been through hell over the last two years. His mom is very sick, and he's paying a lot of her bills. He's glad to do it, but he's running out of resources. He has a commission-based job that was great until the economy tanked. Now it's unreliable. I know because he told me in a letter that he feels embarrassed by this.

"The Enemy keeps telling me I'm a failure," he wrote. "I know it's not true. I know what the Bible says, that I'm a conqueror, but it's like the proof keeps stacking up, and I can't refute it. How many times can I fail before I have to admit, you know what, maybe I actually *am* a failure?"

At this moment, though, Bill had his eyes closed, and I knew it might be the only moment all week when the chatterbox was drowned out by the voices of the thousands of other believers who were singing along with him: "The One who reigns forever, He *is* a friend of mine."

I turned around to grab my microphone because there was only one more chorus before I was up to preach. As I turned, I saw a little hand waving right in front of my face, and I heard my two-year-old daughter singing loudly enough to get my attention over the music of the electric guitars and kick drum: "DA ONE WHOO WAYNS FOW EBWA…, HE ID A FWEND OB MINE!"

Abbey was wailing like she understood every word better than the lady in her twenties, better than Bill, better than the preacher. And although I didn't get superemotional in that moment, because I didn't have much time, I put my right hand on her face and prayed, *God, help her always know this, deep down, that You are the most powerful person she'll ever encounter—and You love her more than she'll ever understand.*

I understand that the culture my daughter is growing up in will wage a war against her security in Christ. The chatterbox will start blaring at an early age through media messages, through images online and in print, telling her she's deficient. It will tell her things about her body that will make her dissatisfied with her shape and substance. It will tell her things about her personality that will make it difficult for her to see God's fingerprints on her constitution and character.

But I plan to teach my daughter how to keep singing that refrain. Or, from the looks of things, she might be teaching me.

The reality that stared at me in the face of each of those people that day was the imminence of God's friendship married with the wonder of hope in His power.

Combine those two, and you have the most powerful force in the universe, more powerful than any words the chatterbox will ever speak to you, about you, or over you.

This is the force of God's *favor.*

Over Saved and Highly Favored

Living within the framework of God's favor reorients you to a new reality.

I knew a woman in college whom I would describe as "over saved," as one comedian put it. Everything you asked her turned into something spiritual. You'd say, "Hey, Mary, I like that shirt," and she'd say, "The Lord told me to wear purple today to remind me that I am royalty." I did not make up that example. Queen Mary said those exact words.

I must admit, I got pretty adept at avoiding her, other than the general Southern courtesies, such as "Hey, Mary, how are you?"

Of course, Mary couldn't answer me by saying she was fine or great. Instead, she'd reply, "I'm blessed and highly favored." Every single time I asked Mary how she was, she replied with the precision of an army recruit, "Blessed and highly favored, praise the Lord."

Now, I'm not suggesting we mimic Mary and make *blessed and highly favored* our auto response for every salutation. But there's something cool about the way she described herself, the way she saw herself.

Favored.

The concept of God's favor has been sliced and diced and served up in so many different ways that it's hard to use it without certain images coming to mind. Images of preachers telling you that if you pray for God's favor, you'll get convenient parking spots and incredible deals on Black Friday, and you'll never be sick, sad, or stuck in traffic.

While I have no doubt about (and no objection to) God's ability to bless us in those ways, these are not the most important facets of God's favor. God's favor is not just a force to make our lives more *convenient*. It's a supernatural reality that enables us to fulfill God's purpose.

I'll prove this to you from the life of another, much more famous Mary. Remember in the Christmas story when the angel came to the Virgin Mary and told her she would have a child and He would be the Son of God? Do you remember what the angel said to Mary in his greeting?

Greetings, you who are highly favored! The Lord is with you.
(Luke 1:28)

Perhaps this is where Crazy Mary got her line. From Mother Mary herself. But look at Mary's response. It's unexpected.

> Mary was greatly troubled at his words and wondered what kind of greeting this might be. (verse 29)

On the surface this is confusing. You'd think that if a messenger from God told you that you were highly favored, you'd be ecstatic. Getting an announcement from an angel that you're highly favored is kind of like finding out that you're in the audience for Oprah's Favorite Things. Or that you'll be featured on *A Wedding Story*. (Do they still make that show?)

In this case, though, Mary's initial response to the announcement of God's favor was *fear*. And as the story unfolds, we see that she had sufficient reason to be afraid.

> But the angel said to her, "Do not be afraid, Mary; you have found favor with God. You will conceive and give birth to a son, and you are to call him Jesus." (verses 30–31)

We have to take a moment to appreciate the irony and absurdity of this moment. An angel appears and prophesies a pregnancy that wasn't the result of relations between a man and a woman and that will prove to be *the* event in world history: the incarnation of the Son of God.

Think of the kinds of doubts and rejection Mary would face over the next nine months and beyond. As her pregnancy progressed, she'd be forced to answer impossible questions from understandably suspicious people. She'd feel the parade of judgmental stares of those who had their own explanations of her situation. *Oh yeah, that's Mary. She's the girl that "God got pregnant."*

They would have laughed in her face and behind her back and done and said much worse than what I feel comfortable printing on these pages.

She'd question herself, surely. *Was that really an angel? Have I completely lost it? And how in the world am I going to raise this child?*

This is what you call favor? And the angel has the nerve to suggest Mary has nothing to be afraid of?

What kinds of insecurities would the chatterbox try to amplify in the mind and heart of the young, vulnerable, and now disreputable Mary?

We get a glimpse of Mary's very human, initially hesitant reception of the news in verse 34:

"How will this be," Mary asked the angel, "since I am a virgin?"

After explaining in very limited detail how the process would unfold and assuring Mary that the Holy Spirit was able to accomplish even what seemed to be impossible from a human perspective, the angel punctuated his pep talk with this promise:

No word from God will ever fail. (verse 37)

Worst Favorite Verse

The angel's response certainly didn't eliminate all of Mary's trepidation, but somehow Mary found it within herself to reply,

"I am the Lord's servant," Mary answered. "May your word to me be fulfilled."

That verse—Luke 1:38—has been my wife's favorite Bible verse since long before we got married. I always thought it was a strange Bible verse to claim as your *favorite*. (I'm not saying it's not a good verse, just that, if you're going to pick an *absolute favorite*?)

But the more I considered the context, the more I appreciated the subtle beauty of the verse. For one thing, notice the sequence. It reinforces a truth we learned earlier. The reason Mary was able to receive the angel's instruction to carry out the activity that was assigned to her was her unshakable understanding of her identity in relationship to her God.

Read it again:

I am the Lord's servant.

So I am prepared for whatever comes to me. Whatever criticism, whatever chatter, whatever lies are spoken about me, whatever internal agony I'm sure to face…

Since I know who I am…

may it be to me as You have said.

The more deeply we reinforce our identity in Christ, the more fortified we will be against the onslaught of opposing voices in our lives. Although the chatter is never going to stop, we can learn to accept that it doesn't have the power to stop us from fulfilling God's purpose in the world. I can't imagine what it was like for Mary to press past her private self-doubt and public humiliation in order to fulfill God's destiny for her life, but that's exactly what she did. She accepted the chatter that came along with her situation—within and without—as part of the price for accomplishing God's great purpose in the earth.

But it went beyond obligatory acceptance. A few verses later here's what Mary says about her newly discovered destiny:

He [the Lord] has been mindful
   of the humble state of his servant.
From now on all generations will call me blessed. (Luke 1:48)

It takes great faith—and a strongly rooted, regularly rehearsed grasp of the favor of God in your life—to call yourself *blessed* after you've just been told you've been chosen for the most unlikely (make that most impossible) assignment in the history of humanity. But that's the perspective that favor enables.

God likes me. He is with me to accomplish His special purpose in and through my life.

Even in a situation that was laden with uncertainty, rife with ridicule, and incomprehensibly complicated, Mary lived by a continual assurance. She knew she was favored. She believed God had chosen her for a task that was beyond her human ability. And she demonstrated how an understanding of God's favor makes God's children unstoppable in the face of situations that seem impossible and obstacles that seem immovable.

I believe we need to emulate the pattern of Mary's affirmation in order to move ahead in the things God has planned for us.

I am…

May it be to me…

I am blessed.

I am highly favored.

I am a friend of God.

And because all of this is true, whatever may be happening to me right now cannot disfigure God's view of me. In fact, the things that may be happening to me will only serve to drive my stakes down deeper. The less I can depend on circumstances to define my identity, the more I must look to the Lord to reinforce His thoughts concerning me and to impress them into my heart until I respond as if it's second nature:

I know who I am.

And as my friend Pastor Craig Groeschel says, "When you know who you are, you will know what to do."

The Flow of Freedom

Obviously, Jesus was born of a virgin only once. So don't try this at home, Crazy Mary. We don't have to worry much about being called upon to conceive and carry a child born of the Holy Spirit.

Still, we should be intentional about learning how to flow in the favor of God because God has placed significant callings inside each of us. If we can't push past the opposing voices that undermine His authority and disconnect us from our intimacy with Him, these callings are likely to become, as Manning says, the "great deeds [that will] remain undone."

How many cycles of predictable yet completely avoidable defeat will we have to face before we get serious about replacing our faulty understandings with a foundation of God's favor? When we neglect this process—out of ignorance or out of habit or because it's easier to live in the predictability of slavery than the responsibility of true freedom—we sabotage ourselves. We forfeit good things that God wants us to have. We no longer receive His words like promises. They begin to feel more like duties and unreasonable requirements.

Isn't this exactly what happened in the Garden of Eden? That's where the chatterbox (in the form of a serpent) dared to speak to the first humans for the first time. He's the same serpent who's speaking today, using the same old tricks, trying to keep us from the victory that rightfully belongs to us in Christ.

But as we track down that serpent and locate his patterns of speech, we become less and less ignorant of his schemes.

Furthermore, we realize that the One we're with is much bigger than he is.

IF THE ENEMY CAN'T
KEEP YOU FROM WINNING,
HE WILL DO EVERYTHING IN HIS POWER
TO KEEP YOU FROM WALKING
IN FULL AWARENESS OF YOUR VICTORY.

#CRASHTHECHATTERBOX

4

Who Told You That?

People don't believe what you tell them.
They rarely believe what you show them.
They often believe what their friends tell them.
They always believe what they tell themselves.

—Seth Godin

ew things frustrate me more than having my words taken out of context. And since I preach multiple hourlong sermons every week, there are plenty of opportunities for that to happen.

The truth is, some of the things I say are sufficiently stupid on their own without being twisted or manipulated. I have no one to blame but myself for these moments, and now, thanks to YouTube, they can be instantly immortalized.

But it's different when someone intentionally misrepresents what I'm saying. I've had people chop up my sermon into sound bites, using my own words to express the opposite of what I meant. This violates my sense of justice, and I feel like filing a lawsuit almost every time. But at the end of the day, I'm just a preacher who often makes mistakes, sometimes out of motives that are pure and other times maybe not so pure. I should probably just get over it.

What's infinitely worse is when the very words of the God of the universe, who never makes mistakes and only speaks from the purest motives, are taken out of context.

This, of course, is the strategy of the serpent, and it's one of the most effective devices of the chatterbox. We see it from the very beginning.

The Shape of the Serpent

When the devil wanted to lure Adam and Eve away from their true identity in God, he did it through the power of insinuation. It was the only way his plan would work. Had the serpent approached Adam and Eve with the offer "Hey, abandon all the promises God has made you, and betray the very nature of the One who gave you life," we'd all still be partying in the garden. Even Adam would have seen straight through, and walked away from, this blatant temptation to disobey God.

Instead, in Genesis 3:1 the craftiness of the chatterbox is fully manifested. The serpent poses a question to Eve: "Did God really say, 'You must not eat from any tree in the garden'?"

It's not a direct temptation—it's an invitation to a dialogue. The chatterbox loves to get you chatting. Once the conversation starts, you'll find it difficult to leave the lot.

Most of the decisions that send our lives in the wrong direction are the result of our wrongly answering the question "Did God really say…?" Since the Enemy can't take away the promises God has made you—about who you are in Him and who He desires to be to you—he hangs question marks over those promises.

In this case he forms a question mark (here I picture a snake curling up to form the actual shape of a question mark—do what works for you) over one of God's instructions. His goal is to create doubt, but he's done it in a way that is so devious it's hard to detect. Here perhaps it would be helpful to take a look at the original, chatterbox-free instruction God gave Adam.

You are free to eat from any tree in the garden; but you must not eat
from the tree of the knowledge of good and evil, for when you eat from it
you will certainly die. (Genesis 2:16–17)

Is it just me, or is there an enormous discrepancy here?

The serpent's question: "Did God really say, 'You must not eat from any tree in the garden'?"

What God *really* said: "You are free to eat from any tree—except this one, because it's not good for you."

Could the interpretation be any more twisted? This is an ideal case study of the basic way the chatterbox obscures our identity. He starts by confusing our understanding of God's instructions and intentions.

The first command God gave to Adam and Eve was not of *limitation* but *liberation*. It's so clear, evidenced in the way the statement begins: "You are *free.*" His motives are pure: to keep them from *dying.*

Yet somehow the Enemy spins it to suggest that God is holding out on you. That's how the chatter starts. *God doesn't want you to enjoy much, does He? He doesn't want you to fully explore your identity. You need to free yourself. Christianity is so restrictive. Explore. Find yourself. Be yourself.*

Credit Eve with this: she didn't fall for the first lie. In fact, she corrected the serpent by restating God's initial instruction, getting it mostly right. But the critical mistake we make isn't usually because we have the wrong information. It's because we engage in the wrong conversation.

I like to say that doubt is like a telemarketer. The best strategy is never pick up the phone.

Did God Really Say...

Once you allow the Enemy to hit you with "Did God really say…," it's unlikely you'll make it out of there without sustaining some blows. Probably not to the extent that you get the entire human race kicked out of paradise. But that doesn't mean the consequences aren't serious.

I once asked a young lady in our church how her lifelong battle with eating disorders started. Was it all at once? Or did an event trigger it?

She didn't quite know how to answer, she said, because my questions made it sound like the boundaries of the struggle were more clearly defined than they were in reality. She said she'd struggled with her weight all her life, but gradually the struggle shifted, becoming less about her weight and more about her worth. In her twenties, when her friends were getting married, she wasn't. What was wrong with her?

Although she didn't use these words, it was as if she was wrestling with the question "Did God really say I am fearfully and wonderfully made?"

One day she realized that she was no longer taking responsible steps to improve her health and appearance. Insecurity had embedded itself into her self-perception. She no longer saw in herself the image of God. She noticed how she would feel a sort of disgust when she saw herself in pictures. So she set out to control and manipulate her body into a form that God never intended. This led her to places so dark emotionally that she eventually succumbed to other, more visible signs of dysfunction. That's when her family and friends intervened. Gradually she started rebuilding her identity in the image of Christ. But the rebuilding came at a great cost to her and to many people she loved.

After she had outlined her journey for me, she offered this thought: "I guess I just let the lies overpower the truth. And slowly they became my truth."

How are you defining the truth of who you are? By whose standards? What subtle lies has the serpent been weaving into your understanding of God's intentions for you? How have they been corrupting your identity? What is that corruption costing you? Peace? Joy? The ability to connect with others who need you to be there for them? The ability to hear from God about His direction for your life?

Replacing the lies may take some time, but locating them is a much more immediate process. That's because you're not searching by yourself.

I love how the Scriptures describe the events following Adam and Eve's sin. In the narrative we hear the first sounds of the redemptive heart of God toward those who have been taken captive by the Enemy's lies.

Adam and Eve, freshly informed of their nakedness as a result of their sin against God, are in hiding. Hiding from, ironically, the God who has no doubt installed a tracking device on His original creation. But in compassion the Lord calls out to the man: "Where are you?"[1]

Yes, the serpent is a master of asking questions to insinuate things about God's intentions: "Did God really say..." Thankfully, God counters those questions with a question of His own: "Where are you?"

God doesn't ask because He needs the information. He knows His way around this garden. He asks so that Adam can locate himself in relation to his God. So the hiding can stop.

Adam's answer is straightforward enough: "I heard you in the garden, and I was afraid because I was naked; so I hid."[2]

And God's next question is my favorite of all. It is the ultimate counter-question, and it's the source of our separation from God: "Who told you that you were naked?"[3]

Implicit in God's question "Who told you that?" is at least part of the answer:

Because it sure wasn't Me.

It's time to locate the lies and the liars—and reject the labels they've created. I believe the voice of God is calling us out of our hiding with a question that at once exposes and embraces us: "Who told you that?"

Who told you that you were unworthy of My love until some future point in time when you can clean yourself up?

Who told you that you couldn't be forgiven of that one sin even while you still struggle with it but desire to overcome it?

Who told you that the way you look is abnormal because of a feature that society may deem unattractive?

Who told you that the skills and gifts I've given you aren't much good and won't make much of an impact?

Who told you that when you speak, people are just waiting for you to shut up, and you never have anything good to say?

Who told you that you are coming up short and will always come up short as a parent, as a spouse, as a son, as a daughter, even though you're growing and trying?

Who told you that you were stuck and doomed to die just like you are because of the thoughts and actions that have dominated your life up to now?

The serpent gets nervous when we start challenging the doubts, dysfunctions, and insecurities his questions have propagated in our lives. When we discover what God has *really* said, we experience a liberation that leads to fulfillment. This fulfillment doesn't simply enable us to be happy, tranquil, and actualized. It equips us to start answering the questions according to what God says, not what we see.

Meet the Press, Beat the Devil

When our church first started growing, we got a few requests for local media interviews. This was new territory for me, so I asked a friend with lots of experience what I should know to keep me from saying stupid things that would end up on TV. He recommended a media consultant.

So we brought in a guy for a day's worth of training. The first part of the day was pretty entertaining and informative, watching clips of pastors saying dumb stuff and feeling glad it wasn't me. In most cases what the pastor had actually said was innocent. But by the time it had been edited for broadcast, the pastor looked ignorant or arrogant and in some cases downright evil.

I took lots of notes, then asked, "Okay, so how do I avoid ending up on your little highlight reel in the future?"

"Well, number one," he said, "be very careful whom you talk to." Eve should have hired this guy.

"But when you *do* talk," he continued, "there are some guidelines that will leave *you* in control no matter what questions the interviewer asks. And that's what the rest of the day is about.

"Now I'm going to hammer you," he continued. "I'm going to ask you about fifty of the most common questions that news media would be likely to ask you. Some of them are straightforward; some are designed to trip you and destroy you. We're going to record all your answers, and later we'll make a transcript. I'll evaluate your answers as we go, and I'll let you know how you did. Sound good?"

"Yeah, sounds amazing, man."

"Great. Question one: Pastor Furtick, what do you think about _____." In the blank he referenced a national scandal that was happening in some other church at that time.

I said, "Well, I think these kinds of scandals are awful and hurtful..."

I had more to say about integrity and accountability, but he interrupted me. "Stop. You're already doing it," he said.

"Doing what? Answering the question?" I said.

"Nope, you're answering *their* question on *their* level. You're letting the question dictate your answer," he explained.

"Isn't that what I'm supposed to do? Isn't that the point of the interview?" I asked.

"No, the point is that, no matter what you say in response to that question, you lose. Because they're going to peg you as an opponent of the other church, and it's not going to turn out well. So when they ask you what you think about what so-and-so church is doing—no matter the details of the question—your answer should be something like, 'We celebrate all the ministry that churches are doing for Jesus Christ, and we pray for all those involved, and our goal at Elevation Church is to do ministry so that people far from God will be raised to life in Christ.'"

"That's it?" I asked.

"Nope. Because then they're going to do a follow-up question, and they're going to say, 'Yeah, but what about the person who said *this* in criticism of your ministry?'

"You're going to want to defend yourself. But don't play defense. Just change the wording a bit from what you said the first time and say, 'At Elevation Church our hope is that we can always do ministry in such a way that people far from God will be filled with life in Christ.'

"Don't ever let your response get dragged down to the level of their question. It doesn't really matter what they ask you. You go in there knowing what you want to communicate—knowing *who you are*—and you just use their question as a launching pad to deliver the content you've already decided to deliver."

I was disappointed. "Isn't that what politicians do?" I asked.

"Exactly," he replied. "And that's exactly what I want you to do."

"But I'm not a politician."

"But it's not about *you* or what you actually say," he said. "With some exceptions most of their questions will be designed to lead you to a place that will get you off your message and will present you in a way that you didn't intend. So I want you to go in *preloaded* with the answers you want to give that reflect and represent what God has called your church to do and to be."

I've never forgotten the training we received that day. The fact is, we've had mostly great media coverage at Elevation so far, and we've worked with some good journalists. But the essence of what the consultant taught me has proven true. When there's a lot at stake and the spotlight is on, you can't afford to allow others who may have their own agenda to lead your response according to the level of their questions.

If it's true when dealing with the press, you know it's true in dealing with the devil. For the record, I am officially not making a connection between the two.

Before the serpent starts interjecting questions, you must already be *pre-loaded* with the Word of God so that whatever he tries to lead you into, you're taking a stand—not on what he's suggesting, but on what God has already said in His Word about the issue you're facing.

Keep this in mind when the Enemy comes to you like he came to Adam and Eve, introducing just a little bit of doubt: "Did God really say…" If you play along with his line of questioning, before long you'll find yourself naked and ashamed. You'll wind up disoriented and disconnected from the voice of God that longs to call you by name in the cool of the day.

Delete and Download

So how, practically speaking, do you avoid playing the Enemy's game? How do you preload your responses according to the Word of God?

No one demonstrates this strategy with greater clarity and conviction than Jesus. Just before He began His ministry, He was tempted by the devil in the wilderness. This is the same serpent we saw in the garden, showing up in a different way in a different situation.

I've heard a lot of teachings categorizing the three temptations Satan offered to Jesus and how each of those categories relates to us.

But my objective here is not really to give a detailed analysis of *how* the Enemy attacked Jesus. I want to go straight to the heart of precisely *what* the Enemy was trying to attack. When you understand what the Enemy's after, you can make a plan for protecting it.

Behind each of the temptations the Enemy set before Jesus was a sort of dare: to prove His *identity*. The Enemy adeptly spun a web of deceit by twisting the very Word of God in an effort to challenge the essence of who Jesus was.

If you are the Son of God, turn these stones to bread…
throw yourself off this mountain…
bow down and worship me.[4]

Yes, there's something we can learn from the nature of each of these temptations. They do seem to parallel "the lust of the flesh, the lust of the eyes, and the pride of life" as outlined later in the New Testament in 1 John 2:16. These are the same areas of susceptibility where the Enemy lures us with lies today.

Here's the more immediately relevant takeaway for us: at the core of every temptation we will face, we're ultimately being tempted to question in our hearts, and then contradict with our actions, our true identity as God's children.

That's what the Enemy is trying to get you to do, and it's the same design no matter what tools he chooses to use. He'll use whatever he can—maybe sex, maybe spending, maybe medicating loneliness with drugs or food or gossip, all of the above, or something else altogether. He'll tell you to turn stones to bread, throw yourself off the mountain, bow down and worship him, or all of the above, or something else altogether. The details matter less than the intent: his objective is to mess with your head until you have forgotten who you are. Forgive me, as the spirit of the lion king is apparently coming upon me right now. But the words are true.

The only opportunity the chatterbox ever has to download lies into our heads is if we have allowed it first to delete the memory of who we are in Christ.

Jesus crashed the chatterbox—in all its forms and functions—by the power of a transcendent, irrefutable declaration:

"It is written."[5]

Each time the serpent sounded off, Jesus spoke a better word.

Adam Reloaded

The story of the temptation in the wilderness is the first record we have of the devil's attempts to lead Jesus away from His mission by interjecting question marks and suggesting alternate routes. But Jesus had seen the whole song and dance before. In fact, it was the reason He came to earth. He was sent as heaven's answer to the fallout that ensued after sin entered the world because the first man, Adam, forgot what God had told him.

One of the ways Paul explains the identity of Jesus is by referring to Him as the second Adam.[6] It's an important contrast. The first Adam was led away from the will of the Father by questions that contradicted the clear word of God. Jesus fulfilled the will of the Father by contradicting the devil's questions with the clear Word of God. Such questions would not and could not work on Jesus. His answer would be the same every time. No amount of chatter could cause Him to deviate from the script in which He was the main character:

It is written.

That's why Satan's temptation of Jesus had no more chance of succeeding than a Guns N' Roses original lineup reunion tour. Because Jesus was *fully* loaded with the Word of God. He was literally *pre*loaded with the truth of Scripture in a way that only He could be: He *was* the Word of God. So Satan's interrogation of Jesus hit a dead end at every turn. It failed that day in the isolation of the wilderness. It would fail in a mob scene that marched Jesus up a hill called Calvary three years later, where scoffing voices dared him to make like Houdini and prove Himself the Son of God by coming down off the cross.

And it failed at every assault it launched in between. The chatter surrounding the identity and ministry of Jesus was nonstop.

Who does this man think He is?

Doesn't He realize He's just the carpenter's son?

Who is this man that He forgives sins?

None of it stopped Him. None of it slowed Him down. Jesus kept moving toward His mission—toward the perfect will of His Father—even when the false accusations of powerful men rendered Him bound and sentenced Him to die.

Even when the masses who had previously enjoyed the benefits of the Bread Multiplier shouted in unison, "Crucify him!… Crucify him!"[7]

Jesus rose above the chatter and the cruelty with His silence—and obedience. In the words of Isaiah, He was "led like a lamb to the slaughter," yet He did not utter a word.[8] The chatterbox blared, but He refused to talk back.

And we're left with a choice. Who will we follow in our response to the Enemy's questions: the first Adam or the second?

Will we entertain the Enemy's request for an interview? Or will we speak in our souls and through our actions the response we've been trained to deliver: "It is written"?

It's a question we must answer again, as if for the first time, every day of our lives. Every moment, really. Every time the serpent calls us to throw ourselves from our rightful place in God down into emotional states, responses, and spiritual patterns that are the opposite of the life God intends for us. Every time he baits us with self-pity, self-doubt, and the kind of self-absorption that factors God out of the equation, we are faced with a decision: Which voice will we listen to?

Snakes on a Plane

Can I be honest? It's the question I have to answer with every keystroke as I write this book. This chapter, for example, is being written on a fourteen-hour flight from Sydney, Australia, to Los Angeles, California. I have been in Oz for a week, preaching pretty much nonstop since I hit the ground last Monday. It was a great trip, but I'm tired, homesick, and emotionally and spiritually spent. The chatterbox loves these conditions. I could almost see the question marks hanging over my computer as I pulled it out to finish this chapter.

You're not going to get anything done... This is a waste of time for you to try to write right now... You're stuck halfway into this chapter, your stories aren't funny, there aren't enough examples, the computer battery will die, and the charger is in the other bag. The blah-blah-blah and the yada-yada-yada and the same old stuff the chatterbox always says.

Then about an hour ago, as I was typing the stuff you read a few paragraphs earlier, an Australian flight attendant walked by. She was nice.

She asked, "What are you typing? You're really going for it, huh, mate?"

"I'm trying to write a book," I answered. "But I'm not much of an author, so I'm struggling."

"A book, you say? So you've never written one before?"

"Well, actually this is my third."

"Hmm. Sounds like you must be a pretty good author if it's your third. You've already written two more books than most people."

It was the simplest exchange. But it snapped me out of the chatterbox-induced funk. *You know what, she's right. I am an author. A published one!*

And I kept writing. That's why you're still reading.

True for You

Sometimes all we need is a basic paradigm shift—back to what we already know is true, what's always been true, but in a way that's personalized and immediate.

Sometimes that's all it takes to crash the chatterbox enough that we can get on with our work, get back to our calling, and resume our relationship with God. And the more of God's Word we know and the more we're reminding ourselves of His truths, the less dependent we become on others to snap us out of our self-induced negative spirals. We can begin to rely on God's Spirit to renew our minds. So we can get back to writing our books, producing our albums, raising our families, loving our neighbors, coaching teams, studying biology, or whatever God has called us to do in any given season.

When your perspective is preloaded with the Word of God, lies lose their power over your life.

But it's obviously not just our knowledge of what is written in the Word of God that causes the lies to lose their power. Anyone who has sat through Bible classes, read Christian books, heard weekly sermons, or even immersed himself in spiritual-development programs, only to find that change is not the automatic result of knowledge, can tell you that.

The power of Jesus's defense wasn't simply that He knew what the Word said but that He knew who He was in relation to that Word.

And here's where a little biblical context can give us great insight. What event happened just before Jesus was tempted by Satan in the wilderness?

He was baptized in the affirmation of His Father in the Jordan River.

The last event before Jesus's first showdown with Satan was the remarkable scene we studied in the last chapter—when the voice of God pronounced the words that have always been and would always be true about the Father's affection for and acceptance of Jesus:

This is my Son, whom I love; with him I am well pleased.
(Matthew 3:17)

It was as if the Father was preparing Him for the temptation He was about to face.

So not only did Jesus know what was true: *It is written.* He also knew it was true for Him: *I am the Son of God.*

Maybe that's what's been missing for many of us. Maybe it's been missing for you. You know what is true, but in some way it has never become true for *you.* You know what is written, but you don't fully embrace who you are and how those two connect.

Other people are meant to have joy, hear from God, and be used by Him in ways that are significant and memorable. Other people are equipped to do good works, endowed with spiritual gifts, and blessed in order that they can be a blessing. It's not so much "Did God really say..." but "Did God really say *to you?*"

Perhaps God wants to baptize you in His affirmation now. To take you beyond a realization that the Word of God is true and into a belief that the Word of God is true *for you.* It is at the intersection of knowing *what is written* and *who you are* that you locate the lies of the chatterbox. Once you find those lies, you can replace them. You can overcome them.

And while we don't have the benefit of being the only begotten Son of God, we are children of the same Father. We have what the book of Romans calls "the Spirit of sonship."[9] The Spirit testifies with our spirit that we are God's children.[10] You can hear it if you listen for it. It is the same Spirit that presided, in the form of a dove, over the baptism of Jesus. It's within you, working for you, all the time, to remind you.

And you know how it goes:

Paper beats rock. Rock beats scissors. Scissors beats paper.

Dove beats serpent.

MOST OF THE DECISIONS THAT SEND OUR LIVES IN THE WRONG DIRECTION ARE THE RESULT OF US WRONGLY ANSWERING THE QUESTION "DID GOD REALLY SAY ... ?"

#CRASHTHECHATTERBOX

SECTION 2

In which we overpower

the lies of fear

with the truth

God says He will.

5

So What If...

I learned that courage was not the absence of fear, but the triumph over it.

—NELSON MANDELA

Discovering who you are in Christ is not a one-time event. It is an ongoing, life-giving, often paradoxical, and sometimes brain-bending experience. Hopefully, we're starting to grasp some of the clear yet counterintuitive teachings of Scripture about the way God sees us. An understanding of our identity that is based, not on what we see in ourselves, but on who God says we are.

God says I am His child, totally loved, and actually liked, by my heavenly Father.

God says I am chosen to fulfill His special purpose in spite of my weakness.

Initially, this revelation of the love of God can be hard to receive and believe. It can be even harder to nurture and sustain. Using any means necessary, the Enemy will attempt to uproot, choke, and scorch our budding understanding of our infinite potential in Christ and our inestimable worth in His eyes.

He has a seemingly endless supply of tools he uses to strip the seeds of the implanted Word of God. We'll talk about these different tools in detail throughout the rest of the book. But whatever tool he uses, and however he uses them, they all operate on one power source: fear.

Fear was the auto response of Adam and Eve after they were deceived by the serpent. As the voice of God called out to locate His children, who had become hopelessly lost in lies, the force of fear was competing for their attention and dominating their decisions.

[Adam] answered, "I heard you in the garden, and I was afraid because I was naked; so I hid." (Genesis 3:10)

This is a crucial insight into the way fear works. After the Enemy has hung a question mark over God's intentions and instructions, fear seizes the opportunity to isolate us and push us into hiding—just as it did with Adam.

I heard you, but because I was afraid, I hid.

We'll never hear God's voice above all the others if we're tuned in to the frequencies of fear. If the lie is the chatterbox's native tongue, fear is its favorite song. And the refrain only has two words: "What if..."

Overpowering fear is the focus of this section. If we're going to put our roots down deeper and deeper into the soil of who God says we are, we'll have to learn to push past all varieties of heart-hardening fears.

As I'm sure you already know, fear is an insidious force that has silenced the dreams and sabotaged the development of so many of God's children. But the confession we're about to activate gives us access to a much greater force—the counteractive force of faith:

God says He will.

Category 4 Fear

I was nine years old when Hurricane Hugo hit Charleston, South Carolina. It came ashore as a Category 4 hurricane, and before it left the state, it had killed twenty-seven people, left nearly a hundred thousand homeless, and done $10 billion in damage.

The thing is, I had to look up all that factual data about those effects of the storm. But there are other aftereffects that I remember as though they happened twenty-five minutes—not almost twenty-five years—ago.

I remember how, just before the power went out, Charlie Hall, our local weatherman, was pleading with the passion of John the Baptist for people to evacuate *immediately.* I remember begging my parents to listen to him and being confused when they tried to explain how our town, Moncks Corner, was not among those that were being told to evacuate. I insisted that we would die if we didn't leave right then. They reassured me, repeatedly, that we wouldn't die, that we'd just have to spend the night in the hallway of our three-bedroom house, and it would be a long and scary night.

To be sure, it was the longest and scariest night in South Carolina history for me, and I can't imagine how long it was for my parents. Because they had to endure not only the thunder and lightning but also the incessant questions of a petrified nine-year-old. It baffled me that my little brother, Matt, could sleep, leaning against the rattling walls in that tiny, pitch-black hallway. Not even the oak tree roused him as it crashed on Mr. Buddy's Pontiac next door. He woke up the next morning, stretched, and asked, "Is it over yet?"

We all laughed. It was over and we were all right.

Lots of trees were down, but that created a backyard wonderland that I thoroughly enjoyed throughout the cleanup process. The power was out for three days, but that meant no school for three days, and the trade-off was, for me, a happy one. A little damage to our home and neighborhood, but nothing irreparable. Massive damage and even casualties in surrounding areas, but what can a nine-year-old comprehend about that? *The storm is over, we're all safe, and school's out, baby.*

What I'm trying to say is, I didn't know anything major was wrong with me until Ryan Haynes called a few days later and invited me over to spend the night. Then I felt it. It was the kind of mule kick you get in your stomach as a grownup when you're in a crowded place, and you haven't been paying attention for a few seconds, and you look up to discover your toddler isn't in sight. Sheer panic. A flash flood of fear broke loose in my heart because suddenly I realized that I didn't want to spend the night away from home.

I gave Ryan a made-up reason that I couldn't come. Then I hung up the phone, wondering what was wrong with me.

"Who was that, honey?" my mom wanted to know. After I told her that it was Ryan and that he had asked me to spend the night and that I had said no, she tilted her head and squinted at me like she was trying to make sense of a map that identified Boston as the capital of South Carolina.

"But you love going over to Ryan's house. He's one of your best friends. Why did you say no?"

Whatever excuse I offered her was insufficient. I know I didn't tell her the truth, because I was humiliated to admit that, for the first time in my life, I was scared to death to spend the night away from home.

"You need to get out of the house, Son. It'll be good for you." (Possible translation: "I need you out of the house, Son. You're driving me crazy.")

"Call Ryan back," she said. "Tell him you'll be over there in thirty minutes. I'll take you."

I desperately wanted to spill it all to my mom—how the idea of spending the night away from home was making me want to throw up, and could we just keep this between us? Instead, I got in the front seat of the Dodge Caravan and rode silently to the Haynes house.

After I walked in the front door, everything felt better. Mr. Gene was cooking chili, and Ryan had selected our teams for Tecmo Bowl and paused it on the kickoff screen.

Everything went great until we turned the lights off to go to sleep. That's when I started to feel very, very sick. At least that's what I told Mrs. Linda when I woke her up and asked her if I could call my parents to come pick me up. The truth was, I wasn't sick at all; I was scared out of my mind about something I couldn't quite describe and didn't have the guts to own up to. I had been lying in the dark for thirty minutes and crying quietly into my pillow, hoping Ryan couldn't hear me. I was convinced that something terrible would happen to my parents and my brother while I was gone and I'd never see them again. I felt sorry that I hadn't told them a better good-bye, and I felt awful that I hadn't been a better son.

If my nine-year-old emotional state sounds irrational and melodramatic to you, just imagine how it feels for me to be typing it, finally admitting it.

Mom came to get me, and I could tell by her questions she suspected my story wasn't 100 percent accurate. Her suspicion was confirmed when, for an entire year, I absolutely could not make it through an entire night at someone else's house. Not Jeffrey's, not Hamilton's, not Ryan's. My mother and I would prep and talk about it before I left, and I'd resolve to get it together *this* time, yet it would always end the same way—with Mom picking me up or someone's dad dropping me off, probably swearing as he peeled out of the driveway, "That's the last time you're inviting that Furtick boy to spend the night." I wouldn't have blamed him.

But I'd come home dejected, each failed sleepover feeling like a dishonorable discharge. I'd see in the light of the morning how silly and unwarranted my panic had been. But that knowledge didn't keep the panic at bay the next time I was alone in the dark in someone else's house.

Gradually, of course, I got my nerve back. And although I don't get invited to many sleepovers these days, I'm confident now I could pull one off without incident if called upon.

Yet my experience of being terrorized by irrational fears did not stop at age nine.

Turn It Out

It's amazing how, in so many ways, my life is still replaying that scene. There are just different characters and higher-stakes situations.

I run from places and people God has called me to. I'm driven away from where God wants me to be by endless what-if scenarios. They may seem more sophisticated than *What if my family is killed before I get back home tomorrow and I have to live without them?* But in actuality, they're every bit as irrational. What's more, they're downright unbiblical. And they severely limit my life and wreak havoc on my relationship with God.

I can't always pinpoint the source of the fear, and it doesn't usually have an obvious connection to a catastrophic event. But I've learned to recognize the sound of its voice when it starts chattering.

I set out to try something I've never tried before, and I hear, *What if you look like an idiot? After all, everyone else already knows how to do it, and you're way behind. You'll probably be awful at it anyway; you're a slow learner.*

I set out to ask someone a question about something I don't understand, and I hear, *What if they think you're stupid for not already knowing that? What if you're asking something that is basic knowledge to everyone else? What if they interpret your asking a question as a sign of weakness or incompetence and lose respect for you?*

I set out to do something intentional and kind for others, and I hear, *What if they take advantage of you? What if they misunderstand your motives? What if they don't even want your help and end up rejecting you? How will you handle that?*

I set out to embrace a new discipline in my life, and I hear, *What if you commit to this and don't have the perseverance to stick with it? Do you really want to take the chance that other people will watch you fail? If you don't try or don't commit to a specific goal in this area, at least you won't run any risk of failure.*

The fact is, fear is both a global and a personal experience for all of us. We fear stuff we can't control and at the same time tremble at the things we *can* control. We fear terrorist attacks and breast cancer. We fear opening e-mails that might contain bad news about our company or extra work from our boss or a hurtful remark from our sister. Whenever possible, we retreat to the safety of spiritual complacency, which is actually the most dangerous place of all.

The fact is, this kind of fear doesn't just go away after a year. In fact, if left alone, it tends to compound, spread, and destroy. Little fears can cohabitate and combine to form levels of anxiety and terror that will annihilate our awareness of the presence of God.

I love the way the Amplified Bible translates 1 John 4:18:

There is no fear in love [dread does not exist], but full-grown (complete, perfect) love *turns fear out of doors* and expels every trace of terror! (emphasis added)

I like it because it's such an active verse and such an accurate description of the nature of fear. "Full-grown love *turns fear out of doors.*"

When I read that, I picture fear standing at the doorway of our destinies, daring us to step inside. I can hear all the different lines the chatterbox uses to intimidate us when we're on the verge of doing something God has told us to do. Fear pushes us around like Nelson bullies Bart Simpson and Milhouse, and it holds a Keep Out sign over the adventure, wonder, and even simple everyday confidence God has called us to experience.

What Had Happened Was

The other day I asked another author what is the most memorable fiction work he's ever read. He told me about the novel *Something Happened* by Joseph Heller. It's the first-person, stream-of-consciousness memoir of a middle-aged man named Bob Slocum, who is unraveling from within.

The book opens with a chapter titled "I Get the Willies." Here's an excerpt of Slocum's internal dialogue:

I get the willies when I see closed doors. Even at work, where I am doing so well now, the sight of a closed door is sometimes enough to make me dread that something horrible is happening behind it, something that is going to affect me adversely; if I am tired and dejected...I can almost smell the disaster mounting invisibly and flooding out toward me through the frosted glass panes. My hands may perspire, and my voice may come out strange. I wonder why.

Something must have happened to me sometime.[1]

What gives you the willies? What is the *something* that *happened sometime* that is keeping you out of the place God is calling you to today? What are the doors that remain closed because fear has posted Do Not Enter signs in certain hallways of your heart? What possibilities remain unexplored because of the endless what-if scenarios that the chatterbox is programmed to repeat every time the motion detectors sense you making a move toward the doorway?

What if I give generously and then don't have enough to meet my own needs?

What if I go out of my way and nobody appreciates it?

What if I tell him how I feel, trying to get the relationship back to a place that honors God, and he turns it on me and it's worse than before?

Since psychology isn't the specialty of this book, we won't get into detailed discussions about phobias, families of origin, or the pathology of fear. Or how our night-light burned out one time when we were four, and that's why we're scared of Christmas trees.

Instead, let's look at the active response 1 John 4:18 commands us to take when faced with fear of any kind. Here, not only does John give us an action to take in order to overpower fear, but he also points us to the only power that makes defeating our fears possible.

Eviction Notice

First, the command. We are not only permitted but required to turn fear out of doors wherever we find it lurking in our lives. The Father is giving us permission to hit back. Therefore, our approach to dealing with fear cannot be passive. Because fear doesn't evaporate. It must be *evicted*. Or, as the verse puts it, *every trace* of terror must be *expelled* if we're going to receive the fullness of what God wants to give us. The spirit of fear is never to be allowed any access or residency in the life of the believer.

In other words, you either *kick fear out* of your heart or it will *keep you out* of the places God has prepared for you.

If you keep handing the bully your lunch money, don't act surprised when he keeps taking it. And if you wait until a day when your fears magically subside to begin to take the steps God prompts you to take—to go on a mission trip, to ask your sister-in-law for forgiveness, to lead a small group in your church—you'll likely wait a lifetime.

I like this Dale Carnegie quote: "Inaction breeds doubt and fear. Action breeds confidence and courage. If you want to conquer fear, do not sit home and think about it. Go out and get busy."

The point is, we don't get stronger in faith by avoiding our fears. What's true about our physical bodies is also true about our spirits: the only way to get stronger is to work out. And we only overcome the paralysis of fear as we take our *next step* in faith. We initiate the conversation; we make the contribution; we show up for the meeting; we obey God in the small thing. And the momentum of each step pushes against the force field of fear, weakening its power to control us.

Of course, while this talk of fighting back may sound noble, even exciting, the truth is, our fears are strong. They've been building alliances and forming terrorist cells all our lives, collecting ammunition and drawing battle lines.

So, how do you turn fear out of doors when the fear towers above you like Hurricane Hugo overwhelms a nine-year-old?

According to 1 John, the only force in the world powerful enough to overtake fear is the *full-grown love* of God. Deciding to take your stand in the love of God in the battle against fear is akin to having Liam Neeson as your dad and telling him somebody's messing with you.

Fear is the bully that stands at the door and refuses to let you through. *You can't go back to college—you're too old. You can't go back to church—they'll make fun of you.*

God's great love is the reality that towers three feet above fear and says, *You mess with him, you mess with Me.* Fear has no choice but to relocate when God's love grabs it by the collar and says, *You're not welcome here.*

It's decision time: Will you hide in the shadows of fear with Adam? Or respond to the voice of God's love as it summons you to fight against fear and press forward into new victories?

God's Favorite Fear

We've mentioned a few of the what-ifs that fear attempts to use in dragging our minds down useless paths and keeping us out of hopeful places. Allow me to mention a few more.

What parent hasn't been seized by the stranglehold of what-ifs set off when the phone rings late and the teenager is out with a freshly minted driver's license? Or when the newborn has a fever, the doctor on call hasn't called back, and the medicine isn't helping?

What single person hasn't felt ripples of anxiety when another birthday has passed and prospects for marriage haven't brightened? When everyone around you seems to be happily spoken for, and the thought keeps recurring that maybe you'll *never* find anyone. After all, you haven't yet.

And what if? What if they don't call? What if they do? What if I don't get offered the job? What if I do? What if the alarm doesn't go off? What if it goes off and I don't hear it? What if I forgot something? What if I remember? What if I marry her and she's not the one? What if I marry her and she is the one but I don't like being married?

The world of what-ifs is a black hole, and it will suck your joy, peace, and hope into its vortex if you venture near its vicinity.

I should point out that considering the implications of our decisions and anticipating their consequences are not bad things. Every time I teach about how all fear is to be eliminated from the life of a believer, invariably this question will arise: "Aren't some fears good to have?" For example, isn't it good to be afraid of getting your foot caught under the lawnmower, texting while driving, or buying a house with a mortgage you can't afford?

Of course we should be apprehensive about things that would harm our lives and be cautious about things that would damage us or others. But I wouldn't classify that as walking in fear. I'd call it operating in wisdom. And it is supremely good to walk in wisdom. In fact, the Bible says that the fear of the Lord is the *beginning* of wisdom.

So in other words, there is only one kind of fear I can find in the Bible that God endorses: the fear of God.

Storm Stand Still

Contrary to certain religious rhetoric, the fear of the Lord is not the fear that God is out to get you. As New Testament believers, we understand that God has come near to us in the person of Jesus and that what Christ did on the cross completely satisfied God's wrath against sin. God will not take out on me what He's already placed on Jesus. So now, because I have trusted Christ with my life, I never have to be scared of God.

What is the fear of God, then? It is being terrified of ever being outside of His protection. This kind of fear works *for* us, just like God Himself does, rather than against us. It can guide us and keep us on track when we're being lured over the edge into courses of action we have no business considering.

But the other kind of fear, the chatterbox kind, is an entirely different genre. And it takes control when I start giving more weight to my *what-ifs* than to *what God says*. When you let the chatterbox take a valid concern, amplify it, and turn it into a consuming noise that is louder than God's voice, the spirit of fear gains leverage. And then down you go, because your heart cannot be filled with faith in God at the same time it's singing the refrain "What if..."

I love the story of the disciples in the storm the way Mark records it in his gospel.

> That day when evening came, [Jesus] said to his disciples, "Let us go over to the other side." Leaving the crowd behind, they took him along, just as he was, in the boat.... A furious squall came up, and the waves broke over the boat, so that it was nearly swamped. Jesus was in the stern, sleeping on a cushion. The disciples woke him and said to him, "Teacher, don't you care if we drown?" (Mark 4:35–38)

The disciples were petrified of the storm, and they had every right to be. There was no onboard GPS, no boat-owner's insurance, and it was *their* boat Jesus had borrowed for this ministry expedition. Their livelihoods, not to mention their *lives,* flashed before their eyes. But finally Jesus "got up, rebuked the wind and said to the waves, 'Quiet! Be still!' "[2]

Did Jesus call for the end of the storm at this point because He was moved by the disciples' pitiful state? Or because He was annoyed that Hurricane Hugo was disturbing his REM cycle? Either way, what happened next was a miracle:

> Then the wind died down and it was completely calm.
>
> He said to his disciples, "Why are you so afraid? Do you still have no faith?" (verses 39–40)

The story tells me that Jesus wanted the disciples to know intuitively what all of His earthly miracles were meant to prove: *He* is Lord—He reigns over earth, sky, wind, storms, sickness, recession—and there is nothing beyond the realm of His authority.

But after He proves this definitively by shutting down the storm, the response of the disciples seems strange. According to the next verse, "they were terrified."

Wait a minute. The storm is over. He told you to stop being afraid.

But as the context reveals, their terror is no longer connected to what they were going through:

> They were terrified and asked each other, "Who is this? Even the wind
> and the waves obey him!" (verse 41)

What happened to the disciples through this event is a shift I believe God wants to set in motion in each of our hearts. You see, when the winds started, the disciples were afraid of the *storm.* But after they saw who Jesus was, their fear of the storm was replaced with the fear of the Lord.

We don't have to fear what we face when we know whom we're trusting in. The only thing we ever have to be afraid of is that we would ever live one moment of one day outside the protection of the One who can command the wind and the waves to be still.

The word of the Lord may be coming to still your storm in this moment.

Maybe when you started reading this chapter, your boat was filling up with what-ifs. But as you're reading, you're hearing a voice that's louder than the storm. And you're starting to realize what the devil hoped you'd never discover: anytime Jesus is on board, the storm is outranked.

Nevertheless, the storms rage on. No amount of spiritual training can keep the waves of what-ifs from coming or can decrease their velocity, at least not on our command.

What, then, shall we do with the what-ifs?

Here's the mistake most people make: they entertain the what-if, but they don't enter it deeply enough with the searchlight of truth.

In the next chapter I will share the counterstrategy that has been very powerful for me at times when I've felt fear starting to stare me down. And I'm not just talking about the devastating fears of things like disaster and death. I'm talking about *daily* fears, fears of vulnerability, decisions that are beyond my depth of experience, interactions with people I'm unfamiliar with, stuff like that. Even though I speak forcefully every week about who God is and what He can do, I often find myself locked in cycles of very real fear. And I've found a way to escape those cycles that, although not a perfect formula, seems to work well every time I put it into practice.

The strategy revolves around three phrases that unlock the cycle and show me a way out. They are

What if…

That would…

God will.

So, instead of just wading into our what-ifs, it's time to dive deep into them and find out what's at the bottom.

YOU EITHER KICK FEAR OUT
OF YOUR HEART OR
IT WILL KEEP YOU OUT
OF THE PLACES GOD
HAS PREPARED FOR YOU.

#CRASHTHECHATTERBOX

6

At the Bottom

It was not the cold that made you want to rush out as soon as you'd jumped
in; it was the unmeasured depth—our fear of what was on the bottom, and
how far below us the bottom was.

—JOHN IRVING, *A PRAYER FOR OWEN MEANY*

Tom and Lisa sit in the same seats every Sunday morning at the 9:30 service.
Sometimes they take up the whole row with all the people they've brought to
church with them.

At the beginning of 2012, I had this crazy idea: What if…we had an old-
school, twelve-night revival to kick off 2012? (Not all what-ifs come from the
devil, you know.) We called the experience Code Orange Revival, and we
brought in some of the greatest preachers in the world. Lines wrapped around
the building each night, and you'd better believe Tom and Lisa were hanging
tough, front of the line, hard-core, night after night.

For six of those nights, their seventeen-year-old son, Riley, was by their side.
But on the tenth night of the revival, Riley was fresh off final exams for the first
semester of his junior year in high school. Tom and Lisa gave their son permission to take the night off.

"Be safe," Tom said as he and Lisa left for church.

From the first time you release your child to waddle toward the playground
until that gut-wrenching moment when you shut the car door and pull away
from the freshman dorm, every parent clings to a variation of these two words:
be safe.

No parent, however, wants to dive into the underlying fear that drives those
words.

What if he's not safe? What if the people he's with aren't safe?

What if something happens and I'm not there to protect him?

Four hours later, when Tom and Lisa turned their phones back on as they exited the building after the worship experience, it was obvious something abnormal was going on. Both of their phones were buzzing and beeping, flooded with message after message. Surely the updates they were seeing couldn't be true.

They quickly returned a phone call from an unknown number. Then, in just twelve words, a state trooper transported the Laymons from the middle of a twelve-night revival to the bottom of every parent's worst nightmare: "Get to the hospital right away. Your son's been in an accident."

Tom immediately called the local hospital to see if their son was there. After being placed on hold, the nurse reaffirmed the reality the Laymons will live with for the rest of their lives: "Your son did not survive the accident."

In that moment, as Tom and Lisa later described to me, life became one giant void. The pain was more crippling than anything they had ever faced. And wave after wave, it kept coming.

Their son died, of all times, while they were in *church*. The church Riley and his father found together. The church where Riley was baptized. The church they invited people to weekly. The church where they had stood in line for revival ten nights in a row.

Now it was the church they were attending on the Friday night their son was killed.

In an instant the sermons that had been resonating in their minds and hearts for ten days gave way to the kinds of desperate questions anyone would ask in a moment like this.

Why, God? Why would You let this happen? Really? During church? Everyone else knew before us. We weren't even able to take the call. He was already in the morgue when we got there.

We prayed for his safety. No one cared for him as much as we did. Why would You take our son?

God, where are You?

Make Him Pay

There's no hiding in times like this. Our internal antagonist breaks through loud and clear, demanding to be heard. But even in our crisis moments and nightmare seasons, God speaks. And our ability to hear His voice above all others can be the difference between the life and death of our faith.

It's humbling when, as a pastor, you watch someone's situation spiral into the pit of hell, and you reach out to help them up, but they're already standing. That's what happened the morning I went to preach Riley's funeral. I wasn't sure what kinds of doubt might be prevailing in the hearts of Tom and Lisa or their fourteen-year-old daughter, Ellie. I thought I was going to preach words of comfort to them. But somehow, three days after the worst possible what-if scenario started shaking the very foundation of his family, Tom still found the strength to preach to me as I prepared to preach to a thousand people in the auditorium.

"Pastor, only one thing matters to us today," he told me. "We want these people to hear the gospel. Please don't hold back. We know Riley had a relationship with God. And we know a lot of these people don't. Please make the devil pay today, and tell these people about Jesus."

At Riley's funeral that day, more than one hundred teenagers made public declarations of faith in Christ.

Eight months after Riley's death, as the Laymons prepared to share their story with our entire church, Tom wrote in his prayer journal,

> God, I am thankful that I did not know Your plan but that I do know You. I see how You have cared for us, and looked out for us, not just when we needed it, but in Your all-knowing way, loved us before we thought we were in need. I will trust You when I do not know or see the end, because You are good, loving, and faithful, and Your ways are better than my best thoughts and intentions. I love You, God, and I want to be like Your Son, my Savior, Jesus, in whose name I approach the throne. Amen.

Holly and I will never forget the raw redemptive emotion in the atmosphere as we stood on stage with the Laymon family the weekend we shared their testimony. There was an unbreakable determination in Tom's, Lisa's, and Ellie's eyes as they raised their arms and clenched their fists as the whole church sang in unison:

Through the storm, He is Lord
Lord of all.

Now I want to ask you a question. How can the Enemy possibly hope to destroy a believer with the kind of faith that hears God's voice loud and clear—even above the most violent storm imaginable?

The Worst Possible Thing

When I think about the Laymons, I think about a parable Jesus shared in Matthew 7:

> Everyone who hears these words of mine and puts them into practice
> is like a wise man who built his house on the rock. The rain came
> down, the streams rose, and the winds blew and beat against that
> house; yet it did not fall, because it had its foundation on the rock.
> (verses 24–25)

The Laymons have marked me and our whole church with an indelible impression of what this kind of faith looks like.

Most of the what-ifs the chatterbox tries to terrify us with will never occur. As I once heard Joyce Meyer say, "Worry is a down payment on a problem you may never even have." But sometimes the worst possible thing you can imagine—or something worse—*will* happen. When it does, what will you find at the bottom?

Tom, Lisa, and Ellie have taught me that even when you go through hell, God is there. Only people who have been to the absolute bottom have the right to report with veracity: God Himself is at the bottom. His voice is there. And when there is only silence, He is still there.

At the bottom of the deepest, darkest what-if imaginable is a faithful God.

Building your life on this Rock, the immovable Cornerstone, doesn't make you immune to storms or death or layoffs or stock market crashes or breakups or the flu. Nor does it pain-proof your heart from the sting of loss, embarrassment, failure, or rejection.

I cannot fathom the pain that will always be a daily reality for Tom, Lisa, and Ellie. Nor can I fully comprehend the magnitude of the faith it takes for them to move forward. To still sit—every Sunday at 9:30—in the same seats where they sat on January 20, 2012, with their phones off as the worst possible moment of their lives occurred.

More than one year later Tom says he still loses his breath at least once a day thinking about all the things he'll never see Riley do—the graduations he won't get to attend, the grandchildren he won't get to babysit, and the place in their souls they'll never find a way to fill.

Lisa says it was months before she could even bring herself to cook a meal without crying. "Riley loved to eat," she said, "and I loved to cook for him. He always came home and hugged me, and the next thing he wanted to know was 'What are you making for me?' I miss a million things like that more than I even know how to say. If I didn't know God, I wouldn't be getting out of bed."

But at the bottom, you see that the same Rock that holds up your life in clear skies is supporting your future when everything around you shakes and rocks and reels.

Even as the Laymons' lives were submerged in mourning, God began to piece together moments that, as Tom described, "provided a sense of peace that we still can't explain."

There is solid rock at the bottom. If you have built your life on confidence in the promises of Christ, then you can dive into your what-ifs, and although you may lose your breath, somehow you keep breathing. Somehow you stay standing through the storm.

Swimming to the Surface

What is your scariest what-if? What doubts and chatter have threatened to drown you lately? Perhaps you've already been to the depths of your greatest fear. Maybe you lost the baby, went through the divorce, or eventually folded in the fight against the creditors. And if you have experienced those things, or your own version of them, believe it or not, you have an advantage of sorts over those who haven't. You've already proven that in your darkest, most horrific, most excruciating moment, God gave you the faith to make it.

I'm not saying you'd choose to go through it again. Neither am I suggesting that God put you through it so He could teach you a lesson. Nevertheless, on your way back up from the bottom, you swam to the surface with a gift: a knowledge of God's sustaining power that is deeper than the most searing pain the Enemy could bring into your life.

I hope you don't hear me trying to explain away your suffering, or the Laymons', or anyone else's. Attempting to do that is, to me, borderline blasphemous. For me to project motivations onto God's heart based on my finite understanding of His will would be not only insensitive but also incomprehensibly arrogant and misguided.

But what we *can* say with certainty is that, when the chatterbox floods your inbox with what-ifs, you have a place to go. You can go straight to the bottom. Instead of trying to avoid your what-ifs, you can dive headfirst into them. Because you know what you're going to find every time: *the faithfulness of God.*

It may feel counterintuitive, even unbiblical, to think this way. After all, aren't we supposed to reject *all* worry and negativity? Weren't we supposed to "turn fear out of doors"? Shouldn't we set our hearts on things above?[1] And isn't that the *exact opposite* of diving down to the bottom of our fears?

Listen, if it were possible to ignore all the impulses of panic and anxiety that come our way, I'd suggest we do so. And there are some irrational fears that we can train ourselves, discipline ourselves, and, through God's Spirit, empower ourselves to ignore. But at other times, the only way to drive fear out is by diving in—and touching down on solid ground.

Play It Out

Here's how I try to do it.

Anytime the chatterbox hits me with a what-if, the first thing I need to do is *identify* it. The trigger could be anything from the inconvenient scenario (*What if I left my wallet at the restaurant?*) to the unthinkable (*What if Holly is late because she and the kids were in a terrible accident?*).

Whatever the what-if is, or quietly as I can, I must assess the nature of the fear. What, specifically, am I so afraid of? In some ways this step alone neutralizes the undercurrent strength of the fear. Instead of being swept away by a vague, unspecified *feeling* of fear, I've identified a fact that is driving the fear. Once I've identified what the fear is, I can objectively look at how it needs to be handled. Is it illogical and removed from reality? Or is it imminent—something I can act on right now?

If so, then the sooner I act, the more effectively I can subdue it. In this way I can leverage the fear *against* the chatterbox. Instead of just trying to *ignore* the fear and hope it goes away on its own—which it almost never does—I've isolated and identified the fear. That points me to an action I need to take. And I'm delivered *out* of my fear by taking an active path straight *through* it.

But what about the fears of outcomes I *can't* directly affect? This is where my strategy might sound a little sketchy, but stick with me. Instead of advising you to *run away* from your what-if, I want to encourage you to play it out.

Follow up your what-if with another phrase—*that would*—and then play it out.

What if the worst possible thing happens?

That would be the most difficult day of my life.

Recently someone very close to me seemed as if he might be about to take his own life. I had done all I could for him, and I honestly felt as though my personal involvement in trying to help him heal was making the wound worse.

I called a Christian counselor late one night when the fears were washing over me so strong and so fast that I could hardly breathe. I told him, "I have no idea what he's going to do. I really think he's going to hurt himself, and there's nothing I can do about it. I'm scared to death."

That's when he took me to the place I least expected a Christian counselor would take someone who was processing such a big fear. "Well, what if?" he asked.

"Excuse me? I'm confused."

"What if he did kill himself? What would happen?" he asked.

"I'd be devastated."

"Right. It'd be one of the worst days of your life."

"Yes. The worst. I have no idea how I'd get through it."

"But you would?"

"I would what?"

"Get through it. You would get through it, wouldn't you?"

"I guess I would. Somehow God would get me through it..."

As I heard myself saying those words, I felt something shift inside. I was still afraid, but not in the same way. My hope was no longer being choked out by fear. Instead I was wrestling with the fear but holding on to a hope that was *higher* than the fear. And finding a foundation that was *stronger*.

The counselor had indirectly walked me through the three steps to overcoming the chatter of terror that had been crippling me: *What if... That would... God will.*

God will get me through this. Somehow. Some way. No matter what happens.

God will be at the bottom, and because I've built my house on the Rock, it will stand.

As it turned out, the person I was praying for didn't end his life. My fears, while not unreasonable, had ultimately been unwarranted. But in some ways I'm glad I was forced to face that level of fear, because I came out of the pit of that experience with a new plan to process my fears, no matter what level they attack me at.

I feel like I'm finding a sort of revolving door I can send my fears through when they come marching in.

What if... That would... God will.

It works with smaller fears too.

What if the car repair bill is more than I can afford?

That would be inconvenient. I'd have to figure something out to get the kids to school, and I'm already bad at getting out the door on time, and who's going to be willing to bring me home after work?

But you know what?

God will help me figure something out. He always has. It might be inconvenient, but it's certainly not impossible. He's parted water before, after all. This isn't exactly the highest degree of difficulty for Him.

Out fear goes, out the door, slowly. And you move on, taking the action you can, moving beyond the feeling of *I hate my life. This is the worst thing ever. Why does this always happen to me?* That's where the chatterbox loves to trap you.

And as we've already seen, this same strategy can work on the *biggest fears* if we have the guts to use it.

What if the person closest to me leaves me? Whom would I talk to, confide in, depend on?

That would be the loneliest season and most devastating blow I've ever had to endure. For a while I'd probably feel like I couldn't go on. I'd feel like a part of me was gone.

You can't be afraid to stare into the pupils of the possibility of pain and see it for what it is. Pretending it isn't there or couldn't happen is like popping a pill but putting off surgery.

The key, though, is not to stay down too long in the potential pain of *that would*. It's like being at the bottom of a pool—you can hold your breath for only a few seconds before you drown. The goal is to *assess* the fear. But *obsessing* over the fear will asphyxiate you. After you've identified the fear and acknowledged the possibility of pain, breathe in the promise. And breathe it deeply.

Even if that happens...

God says He will...

...still be the cornerstone of my life.

...protect me.

...lift my head high.

...restore my joy.

...give me peace that passes understanding.

...put me back together.

...open my eyes to new opportunities.

...lead me to triumph.

...make me wiser and stronger as a result of this trial.

...catch me.

...help me in my time of need.

...hear my cry.

...breathe life into me.

...cover me.

...draw close to me.

...send His angels to comfort me.[2]

The Enemy does his best work in the darkness of our ignorance and speculation. He hammers away with what-ifs in the workshop of thoughts we are too afraid to face.

Take the Hit

A few summers ago I came across a book titled *Feel the Fear…and Do It Anyway*, written by a psychologist, Susan Jeffers, over twenty-five years ago. Although her conclusions come from a worldview quite different from mine, I found myself going, *Yeah, that's totally how it works* over and over again as I read. In fact, she introduced me to the term *chatterbox* as she explained the inner voice that, as she puts it, "holds the key to all your fears…the voice that heralds doom, lack, and losing."[3]

Her solution to the frustration and paralysis the chatterbox creates is "to commit yourself to replacing it with a loving voice."[4] As you've seen so far, my statement of the solution is a little more aggressive. I prefer to think in terms of crashing the chatterbox—overloading it—violently if necessary, then replacing it. Not just with any loving voice, but with the loving and powerful voice of God, based on the promises of the Bible and expressed in the person of Jesus. Hearing that voice above all others is the only way I know to silence the internal cacophony of fear in any of its forms.

One of the most helpful paradoxes Jeffers presents in her book—the one I'm trying to advocate here—is summarized in this quote: "Pushing through fear is less frightening than living with the underlying fear that comes from a feeling of helplessness."[5]

The way I see it, you might have to get hit by the wave of fear—or what-ifs—even if it takes you down for a little while. But isn't this preferable to living with the undercurrent of dread about catastrophe and calamity that is outside your control? Isn't it better than secretly wondering whether God is able to handle the hardships of your life—or more accurately, wondering whether you would be able to handle them with God's help if they happened?

It's better to be ripped to the bottom as we press forward in faith than to stay on the shore, playing in the sand with plastic shovels, never really trusting God. While it's cold and dark and often lonely at the bottom, it's even lonelier to drift through your entire life with silent suspicions eroding your confidence day by day.

After all, isn't the danger of missing out often much greater than the risk that comes with stepping out?

Misinformed Excuses

One of the first times this reality hit me was when I was reading Jesus's parable of the talents in Matthew 25. In this story Jesus describes three men who are entrusted with different amounts of money. Their master is going away for a long journey, and these men have his permission to decide how to invest his resources in his best interests.

Upon his return the master calls the men into the boardroom and instructs each man to produce an analysis of his quarterly returns. What happens next is ironic—and chilling.

The two men who had received the most money to manage have doubled the master's initial investment. The boss praises them and sends them back to their suites in Trump Tower. But you can't have an episode of *The Apprentice* without someone getting fired.

When the servant who was allotted the smallest amount of money comes forward, he has no gains to produce. Only misinformed excuses.

> "Master," he said, "I knew that you are a hard man, harvesting where you
> have not sown and gathering where you have not scattered seed. So I was
> afraid and went out and hid your talent in the ground. See, here is what
> belongs to you." (Matthew 25:24–25, NIV 1984)

Why did the man miss out on the opportunity he was given to increase the value of the investment and participate in his master's purpose? We don't have to guess; he gives it to us straight: "I was afraid."

What was he afraid of? Again, his own words tell us exactly. This man has a certain interpretation of his master's disposition: "I knew that you are a hard man."

And that interpretation limited what he was willing to attempt.

Just as, in the first book of the Old Testament, Adam's fear sent him into hiding, in the first gospel account in the New Testament, this unnamed man's fear produced a hiding of a different kind. He hid what he had been given because of his faulty perception of the one who gave it.

I was afraid—of you—*so I went out and hid.*

Not only does the chatterbox spin endless tales about the awful things that might happen to us. It also creates infinite illusions about the terrible ways God will respond to us if we fail. If we attempt to obey God and fall flat on our faces, not only will we be ashamed of ourselves, but we think God will also be ashamed of us.

So we stop trying and stop trusting. Badly misinformed about the nature of what God really wants from us, we dig holes in the sand and bury our treasure on the beach. At least this way, we reason, the waves can't wash away what little we have. We comfort ourselves by insisting that, while our lives might not be very fruitful, at least we're being *faithful*. The fact is, we've become more fearful than we realize, and it's costing us more than we may ever understand.

This is not God's idea of faithfulness.

Now, instead of turning fear out of doors, we have let fear shut us out of opportunities to use the resources and gifts we've been given to honor the God who gave them. We feel God prompting us to give generously of our time, our talents, our treasures. There are words of encouragement we're stirred to speak and dreams of impact we imagine sharing with others. We sense that doing so would bring about change in us, in others, in our world—for the glory of God. But instead of being compelled by the loving voice of the Father, we become intimidated by the harsh voice of the taskmaster who pantomimes and pretends to be God in our lives. "The voice that heralds doom, lack, and losing."

The old chatterbox.

But the chatterbox plays only one side of the record.

In order to really grasp how important it is to walk past your what-ifs and into God's plan for your life, you can't just count what it might cost if you do attempt to obey God and fail. You must consider the cost of playing it safe in an attempt to avoid what God is calling you to do—and succeeding.

The man with one talent thought he was being frugal, responsible, and faithful by reproducing what the master had originally put under his charge. The master, however, had a much different opinion about how the opportunity had been handled:

His master replied, "You wicked, lazy servant! So you knew that I harvest where I have not sown and gather where I have not scattered seed? Well then, you should have put my money on deposit with the bankers, so that when I returned I would have received it back with interest.

"Take the talent from him and give it to the one who has the ten talents. For everyone who has will be given more, and he will have an abundance. Whoever does not have, even what he has will be taken from him. And throw that worthless servant outside, into the darkness, where there will be weeping and gnashing of teeth." (Matthew 25:26–30, NIV 1984)

This conclusion might seem jarring to you. It does to me. After all, this isn't the sentencing of Bernie Madoff. The servant did nothing wrong, technically. And the master's punishment seems to reinforce the very fear that caused the servant to hold back to begin with.

I was right. This proves it. The master had it in for me all along. Now I really know he's a hard man! That's exactly why I was afraid.

But perhaps this man's perception has become his reality. And in light of the rest of Scripture, we can conclude that this perception of God is grounded, not in truth, but in lies.

What the master had really hoped to be able to say to this man was the same thing he said to the other two stewards: "Well done, good and faithful servant! You have been faithful with a few things; I will put you in charge of many things. Come and share your master's happiness!"[6]

But the fear that stood at the door of the man's mind wouldn't allow him to enter into the joy of the master. And now he is losing it all. Not because the master wanted to take it away, but because the servant forfeited it through fear.

He listened to the wrong voice.

The Flip Side of Fear

What are you forfeiting in your life—*right now*—because of the force of fear pushing against your faith? Because you're listening to the wrong voice?

What intimacy are you avoiding because of the fear of vulnerability or exposure?

What growth is being stunted because you won't embrace a discipline for fear of the sacrifice it will require?

What are you supposed to be modeling for your kids that they can't see and won't be able to experience, because you won't trust God in a particular area of your life?

What healing are you unable to partake of because you fear that confessing your struggle will cause you to lose your standing with people you admire?

You can't get stuck on the question *What if I do obey God and it costs me greatly?* That song will start skipping like a vinyl record, and you'll bob along, never attempting anything of significance for God. Fear will lock you up and swallow the key and then swallow you too as a chaser.

Instead, flip the record to the other side and ask, *What if I don't obey God?*

The joy of my Master is calling, and I fear the possibility of missing out on it much more than I fear whatever discomfort or uncertainty awaits on the other side.

And I'm not talking about adventure for adventure's sake. This is not about going skydiving or Rocky Mountain climbing.

We're talking about obeying the God who invites His servants to share in His mission and His happiness.

The harsh realities of failure that fear projects in our minds can seem insurmountable. But Jesus projects an image of our relationship to God that is very different from the one the chatterbox has been describing to you all your life.

In fact, Jesus said that He would no longer call us servants but *friends.*[7]

And we know His words aren't empty, because His love was proved true by His sacrifice.

> Greater love has no one than this: to lay down one's life for one's friends.
> (John 15:13)

In other words, the worst what-if in human history has already happened. The Master's perfect Servant was hung on a tree and then buried in the earth for three days. Jesus went to the bottom. He descended to the depths, suffering the consequences of all our failures and the culmination of all our fears.

For three days, the deepest fears of all those who had hoped in the Messiah were seemingly confirmed.

What if they sentence Him to die? *What if* this does not end in victory? *What if* the One we've given everything to follow is taken away?

It all happened.

But, as you know, the tomb was borrowed. Jesus emerged from the darkness of the bottom, rising in perfect love, standing in total victory, casting out all fear for all time.

Because Jesus has ascended to the right hand of the Father, we no longer have a spirit of fear. But through our faith in Him, we have been given power, love, and a sound mind.[8]

And because the same Spirit who raised Jesus from the dead lives within you and me, we must refuse to bury our hope in shallow graves of fear.

We stand firm—even at the bottom—in our belief:

God says He will.

And since He already has…

I know He always will.

SOMETIMES THE DANGER
OF MISSING OUT IS GREATER
THAN THE RISK THAT COMES
WITH STEPPING OUT.

#CRASHTHECHATTERBOX

7

What Are You Doing Here?

The amateur believes he must first overcome his fear; then he can do his work. The professional knows that fear can never be overcome. He knows there is no such thing as a fearless warrior or a dread-free artist.

—STEVEN PRESSFIELD, *THE WAR OF ART*

Because the voice of fear is so difficult to isolate, let alone eliminate, many of us assume we have no choice but to surrender to it. But recently I unearthed a scriptural dynamic that has rewired the way I process that voice. As a result, I'm learning how to reverse its effects.

This dynamic is hidden in one of the strangest sequences in all the Old Testament. Let's see if you find it as bizarre as I do.

Elijah was afraid and ran for his life. (1 Kings 19:3)

Normal enough on the surface, I know. Man is terrified. Man flees.

Consider the context, though. Elijah is a prophet and not just any prophet. He's the kind of prophet who has the power to call forth a full-fledged drought at God's command. And when he does so, be assured it will not rain again until he *says so.* I don't care who you are, when God uses your words to turn the rain supply of heaven off and on like the knob that controls a Delta showerhead, that's impressive.

In this particular instance the Scripture records that, due to Israel's collective wickedness, God withholds the rain in their land for three and a half years. During those years of famine and drought, God provides for Elijah miraculously, showing him the precise location of secret streams of water and literally dispatching birds to bring him food—a little program I like to call Meals On

Wings. Furthermore, at the end of the drought, God vindicates Elijah spectacularly—in a remarkable setting.

Covered with dense vegetation, and long disputed between the Israelites and the Phoenicians, Mount Carmel is the perfect venue for this showdown. The premise is simple. All the prophets of Baal—the god who is supposed to be in charge of fertility—will call on him as well as all the other gods in the Canaanite roster who supposedly control agricultural outcomes. Elijah's assignment is much more streamlined—only one God to call on, no supporting cast necessary.

And here's the agreement: The gods—or God—who will send fire from heaven to consume the designated sacrifice will be recognized and acknowledged as all-powerful. The prophets representing the losing deity will be publicly executed. These are reasonably high stakes.

A bull is arranged on the altar, the nation of Israel is assembled outside the octagon, and UFC BC is under way.

After a full day of ritual theatrics by Baal's prophets and no active response from Big Daddy Baal (BDB) himself, the crowd is hissing and booing. In a slow shuffle they migrate to Elijah's side. They aren't yet convinced of Yahweh's power, or even convicted of their sin, but they are desperate for rain. And this man is the one whose words are rumored to have set off this drought in the first place. Perhaps the fugitive preacher isn't mentally ill after all. Perhaps God will prove His presence by validating this prophet, and cumulonimbus clouds will fill the skies once again.

Elijah mounts the podium, the capacity crowd falls silent, and Scripture records the result.

> At the time of sacrifice, the prophet Elijah stepped forward and prayed: "LORD, the God of Abraham, Isaac and Israel, let it be known today that you are God in Israel and that I am your servant and have done all these things at your command. Answer me, LORD, answer me, so these people will know that you, LORD, are God, and that you are turning their hearts back again."
>
> Then the fire of the LORD fell and burned up the sacrifice, the wood, the stones and the soil, and also licked up the water in the trench.

When all the people saw this, they fell prostrate and cried, "The LORD—he is God! The LORD—he is God!"

Then Elijah commanded them, "Seize the prophets of Baal. Don't let anyone get away!" They seized them, and Elijah had them brought down to the Kishon Valley and slaughtered there. (1 Kings 18:36–40)

What better outcome could Elijah hope for? The bad guys are dead. The Israelites are on their faces, giving glory to God. And the drought is effectively over. Just five verses later, following Elijah's prophetic command, the bottom falls out of the skies that have been waterless for more than three years.

Running from Your Life

How will Elijah celebrate this incredible victory? Will he be popping bottles at the after party? Regaling his understudies with the director's commentary on what was going through his mind on Mount Carmel? Negotiating royalty rates on the sequel with Universal?

That's what you'd expect. But a few verses later, we see what he does instead.

He's running for his life...in *fear.*

Fear of what? What could possibly intimidate a man of God of this caliber, especially one who has just experienced miracles of this scale? The answer might surprise you.

A single threat from the mouth of one woman.

Read it for yourself:

Now Ahab told Jezebel everything Elijah had done and how he had killed all the prophets with the sword. So Jezebel sent a messenger to Elijah to say, "May the gods deal with me, be it ever so severely, if by this time tomorrow I do not make your life like that of one of them."

Elijah was afraid and ran for his life. (1 Kings 19:1–3)

Under normal circumstances Elijah's cowering as a result of Jezebel's tirade would be understandable. As the queen of Israel, this woman had a barbaric reputation for not only exterminating God's true prophets but also exacting torturous revenge on anyone who upset the balance of her kingdom.

But these aren't normal circumstances. And Elijah, as we've seen, is not your average prophet.

Now do you see why that simple phrase "Elijah was afraid" is so problematic for me? The same Elijah who was mocking and ridiculing and shaming the false prophets just verses before is abandoning his post and fleeing his mission field.

I'd like to think that if I'd just seen God deliver the kind of beat-down Elijah had witnessed, my response would be a little different.

Well now, Jezebel. Didn't you hear what your husband just told you? What part of "Elijah killed every single one of your fake prophets" didn't you understand? Check your Instagram. Surely your time line is full of pictures of how I carved them to pieces in the valley, just like I cut up the bulls on the altar. You know—the altar that my God consumed with fire? I guess you want a piece too? I wish you would threaten me…

But fear is neither linear nor logical. At the first sign of unforeseen opposition, our pose and composure can come undone. As my dad was fond of saying, "Not even the US Army can beat an ambush." No one is exempt from surprise bouts of terror, not even a world-champion prophet like Elijah.

What do you do when your greatest accomplishments lead you straight down the path of an even greater fear? Instead of summoning his faith and standing firm to see the deliverance of his God, Elijah retreats. And in his escape from his geographical surroundings, he begins to back down from the boldness that has characterized his whole ministry up to this point.

When he came to Beersheba in Judah, he left his servant there, while he himself went a day's journey into the wilderness. He came to a broom bush, sat down under it and prayed that he might die. "I have had enough, LORD," he said. "Take my life; I am no better than my ancestors." Then he lay down under the bush and fell asleep. (1 Kings 19:3–5)

Now I'm confused. Verse 3 says he was running for his life. Yet verse 4 says he asked God to kill him.

Which one is it? Are you looking for life support, Elijah? Or shall God send the angels of euthanasia? One of these things is not like the other.

The more I studied this text, though, and considered the context of Elijah's despair and compared it to similar feelings I've experienced under much less duress, the more I got it.

Although the text says Elijah ran for his life—and I'm sure that's how it appeared—it seems like something deeper is going on. In fact, I'm not sure Elijah was running for his life at all, at least not in the sense we would use that phrase. I believe Elijah was actually running *from* his life.

You see, it had been a long, lonely three years for Elijah. Did he survive the drought? Undoubtedly. And through him God won the battle with a unanimous decision.

But winning can be as exhausting as losing. Sometimes the pressure of success can drain you at an even deeper level than the frustration of failure.

Elijah knows Queen Jezebel doesn't have the power to call on her gods and end his life. If she had, he'd have been buried beside his bull back on the mountain. So it's safe to assume that his greatest fear at this point isn't dying. His greatest fear is living—and having to fight yet another agonizing battle.

Jezebel's threat is ultimately impotent, yes. But that doesn't make it ineffective. Because fear often finds its power, not in our actual situation, but in what we tell ourselves about our situation.

The Jezebel Effect

Have you ever been driven into hiding by a threat that, in actuality, had no power over you? If so, you've experienced the Jezebel Effect. The Jezebel Effect is the mechanism that allows the chatterbox to pump up the volume of the Enemy's threats until they deafen your spirit to God's reassurance.

Instead of preparing for the meeting you have in the morning, or praying about the relational conflict you will be forced to face at lunch, Jezebel will keep you up all night, wrestling with hypothetical disasters in the darkness of your mind. The Jezebel Effect robs you of the time and space that is meant to be reserved for restful confidence in God. What you get instead are exaggerated interpretations of negative outcomes of battles you haven't even fought yet.

Living under the influence of the Jezebel Effect day to day will turn you into a zombie. It will send you scurrying from the cover of God's authority and hurl you under a broom tree with a death wish.

It's not just the unpleasantness of fear's voice that makes it our enemy, although that sensation alone would be adequate motivation to silence it. It's the imperceptible ways that it bullies us until we're running in a headlong sprint away from the story line that God is trying to write through our lives. It barks condescending orders in our general direction until we find ourselves running *away* from our callings, our passions, and the source of our spiritual strength— God Himself.

Thankfully, the very thing that fear seeks to separate us from—the voice of the Lord—is infinitely more powerful and persistent than the threats that attempt to silence it.

Malnourished Courage

When reading a story in the Bible like Elijah's, I find myself thinking, *It's a good thing I'm not God.*

Because if I'm God and you're my prophet, that makes us partners. You just asked me to send fire from heaven, and I had your back. I showed you and everyone else what I was capable of. And now you want to run and hide and start quoting Kurt Cobain lyrics? You're making me look bad, and I'm not so sure I want to be your partner anymore. Yeah, if you punk out on me, and I'm God, I might just take you up on your little offer. You want to crash under a tree and write a suicide note while the nation is on the brink of revival? Because you're scared of one vengeful woman? I'll give you your early retirement package, all right.

As I said, it's a good thing I'm not God. His response to Elijah is the exact opposite of the approach I just described.

All at once an angel touched him and said, "Get up and eat." He looked around, and there by his head was some bread baked over hot coals, and a jar of water. He ate and drank and then lay down again.

The angel of the LORD came back a second time and touched him

and said, "Get up and eat, for the journey is too much for you." So he got
up and ate and drank. (1 Kings 19:5–8)

Not only does God not kill Elijah—He actually *cooks* for him. Not only
does He ignore Elijah's request to put an end to his life and, instead, provide him
with sustenance—He *bakes* the bread.

He feeds him *health* food.

He places it right by Elijah's head, where he can't miss it.

How gracious is this God? I'm encouraged that when He finds us in our
fears, He speaks to us, not with threats of retribution, but with reminders of His
care and concern. When we've become embarrassingly paralyzed by the wrong
messages, He gives instructions for our benefit: *Get up and eat.* This is the essence of what I believe God would say to any of His children who have become
dominated by the spirit of fear.

See, Elijah wasn't hiding because he lacked courage. The rest of his life was a
case study in courage. And if you have been born again by the Spirit of God, you
are not without courage either. In fact, in the New Testament, Paul puts it plainly:

Fan into flame the gift of God, which is in you through the laying on of
my hands. For the Spirit God gave us does not make us timid, but gives
us power, love and self-discipline. (2 Timothy 1:6–7)

As believers, when we feel ourselves surrendering to fear, we usually feel like
our problem is that we lack bravery or resolve. So we ask God to give us more
courage, almost like it's a commodity we're currently short on.

But often the issue isn't a measure of courage that's missing in our hearts. It's
that our courage is malnourished. God has given us the gift of faith and forti-
tude in full supply. But for the gift to grow and rise up and overpower our fear,
it has to be fed.

Get up and eat.

We do not live by bread alone; we must live by every word that comes from
God's mouth.[1] That's true. It's also true that God's Word cannot adequately
sustain you—no matter how prevalent it is *around* you—until you receive it
within you.

God Can Only Do So Much

Nate Silver is a statistician who has demonstrated spooky smart powers of pre-diction (he correctly picked the winner of all fifty states in the 2012 presidential election). He also wrote a bestseller called *The Signal and the Noise,* which gave me some interesting new ways to think about the chatterbox.

I read a *Fast Company* article where Silver referenced a fascinating claim by Google chairman Eric Schmidt. Schmidt has said that, on a single day, modern society generates more information than all of civilization had created before 2003. That fact alone, if properly recited, will make you sound smarter than your friends. Silver's point, however, is that although this flood of information means more *noise* (useless information), it doesn't necessarily mean more *signal* (truth).[2]

My application? We can never hope to crash the chatterbox until the signal (God's Word) becomes louder in our lives than the incessant noise around us that clamors for our attention and depletes our courage. Rather than waiting for more faith to magically manifest, we must intentionally feed the faith we already possess by fanning into flame the gift that is in us. We must eat what God has already cooked up.

When my wife, Holly, leaves town for a few days at a time, she precooks, labels, and organizes plenty of meals for me. The food is healthy, convenient, and delicious. By the time she leaves, she has walked me through—likely more than once—all the items she's prepared.

But something strange happens when she leaves. I revert to the laziest and most self-destructive version in the history of myself. A switch flips, and instead of eating the life-giving things my loving wife has prepared, I can only ingest garbage—the kind of garbage I ate in college. For the next three days, I will choose ramen noodles, even though rotisserie chicken is steps away in the fridge. I will consume two family-sized bags of Doritos in lieu of the brown rice and broccoli. And I do this knowing that eventually Holly *will* call and *will* ask me, "What did you eat for dinner last night?"

And following my confession, I know she will scold me in what I choose to interpret as compassionate indignation: "You know, babe, I can only do so much. I can cook good stuff for you. I can show you where everything is. I can even check in to see what you ate. But I can't *make* you eat what you're *supposed* to eat!"

I wonder if God often feels the same way about us? I wonder if He watches us as we run scared from Jezebels and sleep our lives away under trees of despondency and thinks,

You know, I can cook good stuff for you. I can give you My Word and put it right by your head.

I can create men and women with the minds to develop the technology that will put fifty translations of the Bible on your mobile device.

I can make sure you're born at the greatest time in history, making entire libraries of edifying Christian content downloadable to your iPad or Nook, and podcasts of preaching instantly accessible and freely available for you to stream as you drive to work.

I can put gospel-preaching churches on every corner in your community and surround you with opportunities to serve Me.

But I can't force you to read, listen, absorb, and apply. I can't make you eat.

What's the first thing God speaks to His servants when the spirit of fear has transported us miles away from the place He's called us to be?

Get up. And eat.

Feed the faith you've already been given with the promises I've already provided. And expect the same kinds of results I've always delivered.

Strategic Inflection Points

This tender, direct, and necessary provision should be enough to reroute Elijah and get him back on track. But it's not. The following verses reveal that he continues his tour de fear by heading south—another four hundred miles! Away from his post in Jerusalem, into a cave near Horeb, the mountain of God.

And as Elijah pines the night away doing his best impression of a bipolar caveman, God speaks again. This time he addresses Elijah in the form of a question.

The word of the LORD came to him: "What are you doing here, Elijah?"
(1 Kings 19:9)

This is a remarkably powerful question presented in brilliant simplicity. It's reminiscent of the way God located Adam in the garden—"Where are you, Adam?"—but it's even more penetrating.

It's a question God's Spirit has put before me many times when I've checked into caves of my own. When I've retreated into patterns of isolation, self-pity, and neurosis, I'll sense a voice within me, calling into the cave, with a question that is not meant to be rhetorical but revelatory: "What are you doing here, son?"

Depending on which word in the sentence you emphasize, the question takes on multiple meanings. (Read the following options aloud for maximum impact.)

a. **WHAT** are you doing here? What in the world are you thinking?

b. What are **YOU** doing here, Elijah? Of all people, you? The firefighting, Baal-smashing man of God? I could understand a minor prophet running like this—but you?!

c. What are you **DOING** here? What, exactly, are you accomplishing? What's the point in this?

And (final option):

d. What are you doing **HERE**? I have an assignment for you back there—back at your ministry base—where the nation is languishing, leaderless.

How do you imagine God posed His question to Elijah? With the same tone I address my eight-year-old, also named Elijah, when I catch him jumping on the roof of Holly's SUV like it's a trampoline? With an undercurrent of annoyance? incredulity? exasperation?

The text continues, revealing Elijah's instinctive reaction to the voice and shedding some light on God's underlying motive.

[Elijah] replied, "I have been very zealous for the LORD God Almighty. The Israelites have rejected your covenant, torn down your altars, and put your prophets to death with the sword. I am the only one left, and now they are trying to kill me too."

The LORD said, "Go out and stand on the mountain in the presence of the LORD, for the LORD is about to pass by."

Then a great and powerful wind tore the mountains apart and shattered the rocks before the LORD, but the LORD was not in the wind.

After the wind there was an earthquake, but the LORD was not in the
earthquake. After the earthquake came a fire, but the LORD was not
in the fire. And after the fire came a gentle whisper. When Elijah heard
it, he pulled his cloak over his face and went out and stood at the mouth
of the cave.

Then a voice said to him, "What are you doing here, Elijah?"
(1 Kings 19:10–13)

You cannot sincerely engage with this text and not appreciate the divine
creativity and irony in God's way of communicating with Elijah. Instead of directly addressing Elijah's complaints and excuses, God gives him a command:
"Go out and stand."

In the cave it's hard to hear God calling. The reception in there is terrible.
So God invites Elijah to roll up his sleeping bag and meet Him on the mountain
in an open, elevated space, with nothing to obstruct the signal.

God calls us out of caves because, in our caves, voices of fear and doubt and
dread monopolize our minds. The Enemy can't do a thing to diminish God's
promises—that ability is decidedly beyond the limits of his power. So instead he
lures you into places where your *perspective* of God's promises will be dimin-
ished. He convinces you that the cave you're in is safe, when in fact it's an incu-
bator of disbelief and an echo chamber of lies. The chatter bounces around the
walls until the noise is unbearable and escape seems implausible.

But on the mountain the signal is stronger than the noise. When you actively position yourself in the presence of God—responding to His voice in
worship, confession, and obedience—your perspective realigns with His promises. You are reminded that He's seated above whatever circumstance is towering
over you.

And with both parties finally situated on the mountain, God asks Elijah a
second time: "What are you doing here?"

Enjoy the Silence

The analogies and applications of this encounter are endless. The most beautiful
part of this passage, to me, is that God proved His presence to Elijah on the
mountain. I am deeply intrigued by *how* God spoke to Elijah. Once again, if I

were God (a possibility that is uncomfortable even to write), I would have handled the big reveal much differently. I imagine you would have too. If your mouth had the power to blast the surrounding mountains into rubble, wouldn't you want recognition for it?

On this occasion God doesn't. "The LORD was not in the wind."

Likewise, if you could stomp your foot and make the earth quake, wouldn't that be a suitable way to announce your arrival and reinforce your authority?

Yet Scripture says, "The LORD was not in the earthquake."

Even the fire is remarkable, considering no Duraflame logs or Zippos were involved. Making fire appear out of nowhere, without the necessary tools, is incredibly difficult. Haven't you seen *Cast Away*? If you were God, wouldn't you take credit for this feat in order to assure Elijah it was really you and to get his attention? You know, remind him about the fire on Mount Carmel, hit him with a little flashback?

Still, the biblical writer makes it clear, "The LORD was not in the fire."

Instead, God spoke to Elijah in what one English translation of the Bible calls a "gentle whisper."[3] Another version calls it a "still small voice."[4] The original Hebrew language carries this meaning: it was a *silence that can be heard.*

Regardless of how you render the phrase, it raises a question: If God possessed all these other, much more dramatic means of getting through to Elijah, why would He choose to call to him with something as common as a whisper?

"What are you doing here, Elijah?"

On a more personal note, why does He frequently do the same in our lives? When we're overwhelmed by noise, assaulted by paranoia, and nauseous with anxiety, why does the sound of His voice seem so low that it almost gets buried? Why doesn't God speak to us in ways that are more spectacular—and distinguishable—when we're faced with obstacles that seem insurmountable? Why does the imminence of disaster and the possibility of dejection often seem much more present than the protective voice of God?

If God wants us to hear and know and obey His voice, why does He whisper?

I don't know all the reasons, because God has never consulted me on His methods of communication. But here's how I've come to understand it.

He whispers because He's close.

The Enemy has to shout his threats because, although he can distract and disarm you, he knows he ultimately can't destroy you. He can't get to you. When you dwell in the secret place of the Most High, you rest in the shadow of the Almighty. He can't touch you there. He can only forecast fear into your future. Yet God is your *very present* help in times of trouble, and each one of your days has been ordained.[5]

Jezebel shouts her lies because she has no other weapon. It's her last resort, because her doom is impending.

God whispers His truth because He has no need to shout.

In Jesus, our Emmanuel, God has come close, and fear has been conquered, along with death, hell, and the grave.

Greater is He who is in you than he who is in the world.[6] And the One within you doesn't counterattack the foes around you by shouting louder but by drawing closer.

The psalmist spoke with this same confidence:

The LORD is my light and my salvation—
whom shall I fear?
The LORD is the stronghold of my life—
of whom shall I be afraid? (Psalm 27:1)

The key is training your mind to know the difference between the Enemy's threats and God's whispers—and conditioning your heart to respond accordingly.

The Enemy's threats are embedded in lies.

God's whispers are rooted in truth.

The Enemy's threats are designed to paralyze.

God's whispers are empowered to mobilize.

The Enemy's threats condemn vaguely (a reality we'll address in depth in the next section).

God's whispers instruct specifically.

The Enemy's threats conspire to diminish hope.

God's whispers empower change.

The Enemy's threats are aimed to take you out.

God's whispers speak a better Word to keep you in and move you forward.

The secret to overpowering the spirit of fear is recovering the signal, then attuning your spirit to the One who is always speaking. His voice resounds, not at 210 decibels like a blast of TNT, but in a silence that can be heard if you have ears to hear.

And He says things like,

I've got this one, just like the last one.

Trust in Me with all your heart. Stop leaning on your own understanding.

We'll make it to the other side of this valley. We're just passing through.

You can carry on and rise again in My name.

I have clothed you with strength, and I will never forsake you.

I've numbered the very hairs on your head.

That last one is quite an intimate image. You can't number someone's hairs, one by one, from a distance.

You have to be up close and personal to do that.

Close and Capable

I wonder what things God wants to whisper to you right now that the noise in the cave has been causing you to miss.

Try again.

Don't hold back.

You're closer than you think.

Nothing is wasted.

Or maybe this promise from the prophet Isaiah is what you need to hear at this moment to fortify your faith and stir your courage:

> "No weapon forged against you will prevail,
>   and you will refute every tongue that accuses you.
> This is the heritage of the servants of the LORD,
>   and this is their vindication from me,"
>
>   declares the LORD (Isaiah 54:17)

Of course the weapons will attack you—that's what they're designed to do. And Jezebel will shout louder. Her volume is compensating for the emptiness of her defiance. But one word from God, when whispered into your soul and received with faith-filled resolve, crashes the chatterbox. God's promise refutes the tongues that accuse you and vindicates you on the mountain, in the presence of a God who is *close*—and capable.

What do you do when the Jezebel Effect starts running your life—in the wrong direction?

Get up and eat God's Word.

What do you do when the noise seems louder than the signal?

Go out and stand in God's presence.

But don't get too comfortable on the mountain, oohing and aahing at the fireworks, whispering sweet nothings back to God. This ain't a romcom.

God's final instruction to Elijah involves an about-face and a definitive course of action:

> The LORD said to him, "Go back the way you came, and go to the Desert of Damascus. When you get there, anoint Hazael king over Aram. Also, anoint Jehu son of Nimshi king over Israel, and anoint Elisha son of Shaphat from Abel Meholah to succeed you as prophet. Jehu will put to death any who escape the sword of Hazael, and Elisha will put to death any who escape the sword of Jehu. Yet I reserve seven thousand in Israel—all whose knees have not bowed down to Baal and whose mouths have not kissed him."
>
> So Elijah went from there and found Elisha son of Shaphat. He was plowing with twelve yoke of oxen, and he himself was driving the twelfth pair. Elijah went up to him and threw his cloak around him. (1 Kings 19:15–19)

In other words, *Now that you've heard My voice, Elijah, and witnessed My presence and acknowledged your fears and fed your faith, it's time for us to get back to work.*

Go back the way you came. Follow the instructions I laid out, step by step.

I can imagine the conversation between Elijah and God as the Lord's plan was more clearly revealed.

"Wait, Lord. You mean You already have a plan worked out for this situation I'm facing?"

Yep.

"And You've already assigned a successor to carry on the work when my time is done?"

That's right.

"And You've already drawn up a strategy for the downfall of my enemies?"

Absolutely. Just like Carmel. Remember Mount Carmel, Elijah?

"Yep."

Remember how I helped you single-handedly defeat eight hundred fifty false prophets on Mount Carmel?

"Absolutely."

Well, I'm the same God on this mountain—Mount Horeb—as I was on that mountain, Mount Carmel.

I was the same God while you were sleeping in the cave that I was while you were being sustained at the Kerith Ravine during the drought.

Don't let a battle that you are afraid to fight keep you from a victory that's already won.

Go back the way you came. Get back to work.

I don't change, and neither do My promises.

"You mean, I have nothing to be afraid of?"

Not a thing.

"You mean, I'm not alone?"

You never have been. You never will be.

"Well, then...what am I doing here? I believe I'm running late for an appointment with Jezebel."

GOD WHISPERS BECAUSE HE'S CLOSE.

#CRASHTHECHATTERBOX

SECTION 3

In which we overpower

the lies of condemnation

with the truth

God says He has.

8

Finishing the Devil's Sermons

I must be taken as I have been made. The success is not mine, the failure is not mine, but the two together make me.

—CHARLES DICKENS, *GREAT EXPECTATIONS*

f you had to describe the devil's main activity in one word, what word would you use? *Temptation?* He certainly does plenty of that.

Earlier we looked in depth at how the serpent tempted Adam and Eve in the garden, successfully. We also saw how he tempted the Son of God in the wilderness, unsuccessfully. Yet I don't think temptation is the devil's main activity or his most deadly weapon.

In the last book of the Bible, the apostle John gives an eyewitness preview of the epic battle between good and evil. In that account he calls Satan by a name that isn't found anywhere else in the Bible: the accuser.[1] Packed tightly into that one-word title is a revelation of the most devastating game the Enemy plays with the hearts of God's children.

Satan's main job isn't temptation. It's *accusation.*

Now, of course, temptation and accusation operate in partnership. You might think of them as a diabolical tag team, hell's rendition of Beautiful Bobby Eaton and Sweet Stan Lane—the Midnight Express. When the two work in tandem, the one-two punch they deliver can paralyze even the strongest saints.

At the beginning of this book, where we laid out the ways that chatter sabotages our lives with God, we established biblically that the Enemy of our souls is nothing if not a liar. If he's talking, he's lying—that's the way I heard one country preacher put it. But there's a nuance to this you should be aware of.

The Enemy's lies are often powered by truth.

And if we're not conscious of this, we'll misappropriate endless time and energy internally arguing with the devil. And that never works. In fact, it usually backfires.

I used to try to argue with the devil when he started stacking thoughts of condemnation against me. But I found the arguments counterproductive. Anytime I'd start feeling a steady, toxic buildup of guilt about something, I'd try to minimize the guilt by rationalizing within myself how whatever it was wasn't *that* bad. But that would only plunge me deeper into an abyss of accusation. Because for every excuse I could concoct about why my sin or shortcoming was justified, another valid source of shame would pop up in its place. The result was a never-ending downward spiral of internal dialogue. The chatterbox knows how to filibuster even a long-winded preacher like me.

But one day as I was being pummeled in the familiar cycle of condemnation → justification → accusation → exasperation, I stumbled upon a much more effective way to fight back. I remember exactly where I was (in my front yard) and what I was doing (cussing at packing peanuts) when it started.

Before you judge me, hear me out.

Christmas Apocalypse

The Christmas season is supposed to be a time of joyful family chaos. But for me as a preacher, it's more like a spiritual decathlon. In the three days leading up to Christmas, I preach at least ten times for our worship experiences at Elevation. And these are not little Advent sermonettes. They are ten, full-throttle, preach-as-if-it's-somebody's-last-time-to-hear-the-gospel sermons—delivered back to back. It's a great privilege, and God does amazing things each year, but it leaves me feeling wrecked physically and somewhat catatonic emotionally.

Holly is empathetic and doesn't expect too much of me come Christmas Day. She knows that, given the condition I'm in, I'm doing good to smile for a few pictures, stare amicably at walls, and avoid flipping out on a few distant relatives. It's my little way of saying, "Happy Birthday, Jesus." Normally, though, we manage the season and make some good memories even if I am too fried to remember most of them. We have pictures to prove it.

A few Christmases ago we were feeling slightly adventurous. So rather than staying home and enforcing our typical seventy-two-hour, post-church recovery period, we made the drive to Holly's parents' house the day after Christmas. We did decide, though, that it might be better to take separate vehicles. Yes, the trip was only two hours, but when my nerves are this shot, two hours with three small, very vocal children can be hazardous to my Christmas spirit.

Holly left ahead of me, taking the two most, shall we say, *noticeable* kids with her. Graham—the quiet one—and I stayed behind, planning to leave in just a couple of hours. We did half of a P90X chest-and-back workout together—Graham doing a modified version, appropriate for age four. And even though my intensity was far from world class, the serotonin was doing its thing. I started feeling pretty happy. I began reflecting on all the people who had given their lives to Christ in our church over the last several days. I started thinking about how blessed I was to be a dad, a husband, and a pastor. I even started singing "Hark! The Herald Angels Sing," stopping only because I had to explain to Graham who Herald was.

By the time I'd thrown the duffel bags into the backseat of my Maxima beside Graham and started backing out the driveway, I was feeling downright jolly. The sky was ominously dark with clouds, and the wind was really picking up, but I was in a good mood—I was making the season *bright,* all right. Then I saw the empty milk jug in the grass, beside the empty shoebox, beside the empty pie tin. And these items, along with at least two dozen others, were blowing around in the wind—not artistically, like *American Beauty*'s plastic bag, and not poetically, like Bob Dylan's answers. Rather, the contents of an entire Christmas's bags of trash had been, and were currently being, strewn across our yard.

It looked as if a tornado and a team of fifty raccoons had joined forces to see how badly they could wreck one man's lawn.

Before she left, Holly had stacked what looked like every single box in our house—each filled to the top with garbage—beside our two overflowing waste receptacles and left them at the curb. Trash collection was three days away, but we wouldn't be back by then. So Holly was thinking ahead, wanting to make sure we returned to a trash-free home. What she had failed to do was check the weather forecast. And unwittingly, she had left me to deal with this unnatural disaster.

I was relatively irritated by this point. All the nice thoughts were fading fast, and the naughty ones were starting to gain momentum. Nevertheless, this was a time for action, so I jumped out of the car, unbuckled Graham, and enlisted his help.

"Hurry, boy! Grab the trash as fast as you can, and put it in the garage."

He complied, and we hustled at it. But quickly we realized how futile this was. By the time we collected a few items and got them under shelter, tropical storm Yuletide had blown ten times more garbage into the front yard, the backyard, and the neighbors' yards. I saw only one possible solution.

There was a *huge* box that hadn't blown away yet, and it looked empty. It was wedged between a trash can and some of the other boxes. I made a plan to pick it up and flip it over on top of the other, smaller boxes. I figured it would put a lid on the damage and buy me some time.

But as I was picking it up, I discovered something a little too late. The box that appeared to be empty was half full of packing peanuts. At least it had been half full before I flipped it over. Now the packing peanuts were joining the party on Mount Trashmore, formerly known as the Furticks' front yard.

At this turn of events, even Graham's childlike optimism began to give way.

"Oh man, you gotta be *kidding* me. This is gonna take *forever*!" he wailed. "We'll *never* get done now! *THIS IS HOR-RI-BLE.*"

And suddenly I went from being annoyed at the situation to being *infuriated* with Holly. "What was she thinking?" I screamed. "How stupid could you be?"

"Yeah, what was she thinking?" Graham echoed. "This is *STUPID*!"

Uh-oh. He wasn't supposed to hear that.

But I was too far gone now to care what he heard or didn't hear.

Hundreds of packing peanuts were swirling around in an apocalyptic variation of snowfall. And one day I'll appreciate the humor in how Graham had just told me during our workout that he wished we could have had a white Christmas.

But in that moment, hopelessly overwhelmed by the trash storm, I did the only thing I could think of.

I called Holly. And I unloaded on her.

"Guess what I'm doing?!" I demanded.

She inferred from my tone that I was not finishing off the fudge.

I didn't give her time to respond.

"I'm *running* around the *yard* like an *idiot*! Because *somebody* thought it would be a great idea to set out the *trash* right before a *storm*! And *now* every piece of trash we've ever thrown away in our *lives* is *blowing all over the blasted* [not my actual word] *yard*!"

She explained how the weather was calm when she left and how sorry she was, but I wasn't trying to hear any of it.

Suddenly I found myself doing something I hadn't done in more than ten years of marriage. I screamed a stream of profanity—the big ones. I was scream-ing—not *at* Holly, but *to* her—as if this qualification makes it any better. And without even hanging up, in one last dramatic gesture of frustrated manhood, I slung my iPhone across the yard.

It landed somewhere between a coat hanger and a Diet Mountain Dew can.

I screamed the worst word again, at the top of my vocal range.

I looked down because Graham was pulling on me, and he wanted to know what *that* word meant.

One-two.

The chatterbox had done it again.

Soundtrack of Shame

I had managed to fully indulge the temptation to throw a temper tantrum. In front of my little boy.

And as soon as I was worn-out from my temper tantrum, condemnation rushed to mount me as I fell to the mat. It was time for a little ground and pound. Sin had set the ball—now it was time for shame to spike it.

Two days ago you were preaching to thousands of people, telling them about Jesus. Now you're screaming expletives at packing peanuts. In front of your son.

What kind of dad are you? You're a lunatic. You're just like your dad. Look what you just passed on to your son. He'll remember this for the rest of his life.

What kind of husband are you? What does Holly think about you right now? What if her family heard you? What do they think?

They probably think you're a jerk and a hypocrite, and they're right.

You're worse than that. You're a monster.

You can't even pick up trash. You are trash!

In the outward silence and internal cacophony of my own humiliation, it took me about thirty minutes to get the yard as clean as it was going to get. The HOA would just have to fine me or hang me or whatever they do to riffraff like me. I was done, and I was easing out of the neighborhood, heading toward the interstate.

Graham was playing his DS with his earbuds in, and I was desperately trying to divert my mind. But the kinds of thoughts I had in the yard—and much uglier ones—were flying in every direction just like storm-tossed packing peanuts.

I had approximately two hours of drive time ahead of me, and I knew that even if I turned the music up as loud as it could go, the chatterbox would still be my soundtrack. I could have pulled up a sermon podcast or something, but I didn't deserve to listen to God's Word right then. It would have only made me feel worse.

Because I had gone from being annoyed with the situation, to infuriated with my wife, to disgusted with myself.

How will I explain this to Holly? I wondered. And the questions kept coming. *How could she love someone as volatile as me? What should I say to Graham? How can I look him in the eye after he watched me act like that? How can I preach to others when I can't control myself? What's wrong with me? Why can't I change? Ever? How have I managed to ruin Christmas over something so small?*

I started to combat each of these questions with a quick mental argument, even a defense:

It wasn't really that bad.

You're just tired, that's all.

Graham's just a kid, and he's gonna hear those words someday anyway.

But none of this was working. I still felt like the worst person in the world. And none of it was driving me toward God. I was only feeling more and more distant from Him with every mile and every excuse.

Then somewhere on I-85 between Charlotte and Greenville, I had a breakthrough moment. It changed the way I heard the chatterbox as it was going off on me.

Suddenly a new strategy occurred: *Go with it.*

After all, it wasn't as if there was no truth to what I was feeling. It was the *conclusions* that were killing me.

The Truth but Not the Whole Truth

The devil wasn't telling me outright lies—he was just giving me half the truth.

And the best thing I could do was not to ignore the reality or justify my sin. I just needed to finish the sermons the devil had started to preach to me.

In other words, I needed to acknowledge the substance of my sin. But then I needed to allow the Holy Spirit to take my guilt to a redemptive place.

My attitude *was* terrible. The way I spoke to my wife *was* unacceptable. And I *did* need to apologize.

The example I set for my boy *was* a destructive one, and if I kept modeling this, he would likely emulate me one day in his own parenting.

I *did* need to ask God to change me, and I had to take seriously the responsibilities He'd given me.

But even through all this, I sensed God revealing to me: *The devil is only giving you one side of the argument. He's singing you verse after verse after verse, but he's not letting you hear the chorus.*

For example, he's exaggerating the current reality. Your wife doesn't hate you. She knows you and loves you, and she will be more than willing to forgive you.

Your son isn't now fated to be a sociopath. You'll get plenty of other chances to show him a better way to handle pressure. You can even talk to him about it. Tell him how you were wrong. Show him what humility looks like. Flip the script on what the Enemy meant for evil—let Me use it for something good.

In other words, the Holy Spirit was prompting me: *Take the first half of the equation the Enemy is presenting to you, insert grace and truth in the middle of it, and you'll discover a much different outcome.*

In my heart I began to repent for my sinful and embarrassing debacle in the front yard. But as I did, I also affirmed that God loved me just as much while I was swearing at soda cans the day after Christmas as He did while I was preaching about the wise men from the gospel of Matthew on Christmas Eve.

In the yard my actions didn't reflect God's love. But they didn't weaken it or make it go away, either. Because it's not a love based on what I do. It's a love based on what Jesus has done. The Scripture says, after all, that Jesus came into the world to *save sinners.* I definitely fit that category. When you look at it this way, I guess, technically, Jesus isn't the reason for the Christmas season at all—I am. And you are too. The reason He came was to redeem people just like us. And He redeems us in the middle of our mess, not after we get it all cleaned up.

I knew all this on a theoretical level. But I needed to apply it personally and presently, not in a sermon to others, but in a sermon to *myself.* It was a sermon the chatterbox may have started, but I was determined it was a sermon God's Word was going to finish. The Enemy may have *a* word. But he doesn't have the *last* word. I'd heard that cliché before, even used it in messages before. This time, though, the message was mine to deliver—and receive.

As I evaluated my sin in this light, it didn't make me feel completely better all at once. I didn't break out into verse four of "Hark! The Herald Angels Sing." But gradually I did begin to recapture my appreciation for God's unfailing love.

And I started to suspect that the devil didn't like this one bit. With God's help I was turning the tables on condemnation, reversing its stranglehold on my soul.

For the rest of my drive, I can honestly say I felt as though I had beaten condemnation at its own game. This was something I could recover from and learn from.

Of course, I would have preferred to have never thrown the fit in the first place. Ideally, I'd have seized the *kairos* moment and done a Holy Ghost Christmas rain dance with Graham. I'd have made up a song with him about how Jesus cleans up all the trash in our lives and would have woven in some anti-litter messaging. I'd have set it to the tune of "Rudolph," substituting the names of the apostles in the place of Dasher and Dancer and Prancer. Most important, I'd have Instagrammed Graham during the cleanup effort, using hashtags like #daddyslittlehelper and #InstaGraham.

Would have. Could have. Should have.

This is the language of condemnation underscored by the passivity of regret.

It's a dead language.

The thing is, you can't un-sin. You can only repent.

And every time you do, you find that God doesn't leverage our sins against us like the chatterbox does. His *kindness* leads us to repentance. He leverages grace against our sin to bring us to deeper dependency upon Him.

Furthermore, even though there are consequences for our sins, they're usually not as irreversible as the chatterbox would have us believe. Even when the damage is severe, God's grace is sufficient to rebuild us. To modify something I heard my friend Brian say in a sermon: The chatterbox takes what is glorious and ruins it. But God takes what is ruined and turns it into something glorious.

When I finally arrived at my in-laws' home that day, there was no firing squad. Only macaroni and cheese alongside the honey-baked ham.

I apologized to Holly. I told her I was wrong and really out of line. I was so sorry for being mean to her when she had only been trying to be extra helpful. I could tell she felt hurt—which I hated—but I could also tell it wasn't going to be the end of the world or a permanent mark on our marriage record. She is much too mature to judge my character on just one incident. She didn't erase from her memory all the times I *have* responded to tough situations in a Christlike way just because of this one time I didn't.

She forgave me, and thankfully my outburst didn't ruin Christmas in Whoville after all.

P.S. As an experiment, I just summoned Graham, who is now six years old, out to the porch. I read him this story out loud for a quick fact check. I was anxious to see how much he recalled and exactly how he recalled it. He says he remembers the packing peanuts. But he doesn't remember the bad words or the flying iPhone. He giggled when I read his lines.

But he did have one thing to add: "You know what I remember, Daddy? I remember how bad I had to use the bathroom while we drove to DeeDee and Pa's. Do you remember that?"

I'm not saying it's no big deal to freak out in front of your kids or disrespect your wife. And I'm aware that the incident I just relayed is only one example of one kind of sin and the shame that resulted from it. To some it may seem like a mild infraction with a relatively happy ending. (*Is that the worst thing you've ever done? Peanuts, bro.*) Let me assure you, it's not the worst thing I've done, said, or thought. It's just one snapshot for the purpose of analysis.

On the other hand, those who don't struggle much with rage or anger might find my actions appalling and unforgivable. A preacher using foul language in front of his child might be enough reason to burn this book and lose all interest in any further insight I have to offer.

I'd understand.

But we each have our garbage. Some seems to be heaped higher and smell stronger than others. It depends on your vantage point. To God, sin is sin. We all fall short.

The point is, regardless of our particular variety of temptation and condemnation, the Enemy wants to magnify our failures to the millionth power with his exaggerations so he can pervert the power of the Spirit's conviction. Ignoring the Enemy's accusations is impossible. Besides, we don't want to minimize the nature or ramifications of sin. But we must develop the habit of separating our sense of worth from our appraisal of our behavior. It's the only way we can rightly deal with our sin practically, confident in the fact that God has already *dealt* with it eternally. Now He deals with us, not according to what our sins deserve, but according to what His love decided—on the cross.

I relate so much to this observation by theologian A. W. Pink: "The great mistake made by most of the Lord's people is in hoping to discover *in themselves* that which is to be found in Christ alone."[2]

A believer who is equally convinced of these two realities—sin is serious, but Christ is enough—is the Enemy's worst nightmare.

You Are Also Right

In seminary one of my professors told me about a clever scene in the film adaptation of *Fiddler on the Roof.*

Tevye, the key figure, is delivering milk to the villagers. In a conversation that follows, one of the townsmen, Avram, tells the others that Jews in a nearby village were expelled from their homes.

One of the men says, "Why should I break my head for the outside world? Let the outside world break its own head."

Tevye agrees, "He is right."

At that point a young man named Perchik, an outsider, steps up and says, "Nonsense. You can't close your eyes to what's happening in the world."

Tevye replies, "He is right."

Avram answers back, pointing out the obvious contradiction: "He's right *and* he's right? How can they *both* be right?"

Smirking, Tevye responds, "You know, you are *also* right."[3]

I find myself, as the apostle Paul did in Romans 7, caught in a contradiction. I hear the things God has spoken about me, and I want so badly to believe them. I want to believe that I'm filled with the Spirit, as He says I am. But if I'm filled with the Spirit, why am I so often led by my selfishness? Why are my motives constantly compromised by socially acceptable expressions of envy and subtle manifestations of greed? If what God says about me is right, why can't I *live* the way I claim to believe?

That's when the other voice speaks up—the voice of condemnation. *This stuff you believe about how you're filled with the Spirit is a lot of hocus-pocus, isn't it? If not, why isn't it working for you? Even your good deeds aren't as good as you would have others believe. If you're filled with the Spirit, why would you* [insert recent act of selfishness—we all have plenty to choose from]*? And if you're really a follower of Christ, then why wouldn't you* [insert recent missed opportunity to glorify God]*?*

I have God's Word telling me I'm seated with Christ in heavenly places, free from blame and clear of accusation, a new creation, a changed man, by the power of Jesus.

On the contrary, I've got the chatterbox accusing me of all kinds of short-comings—all the ways my heart is incongruent with God's Word, all the old habits that still persist in my daily life. And the worst part about this chatter is that so much of it is *true*!

I want to shout with the villager Avram: *They can't both be right!*

And the dilemma is even more complicated. Because I've spent so much of my life consumed by the voice of condemnation, my ability to distinguish is corrupted. How can I tell condemnation from conviction?

Like any thief, no matter how skilled or experienced, condemnation always leaves a few clues at the crime scene.

You just have to know where to look.

A BELIEVER WHO IS EQUALLY CONVINCED OF THESE TWO REALITIES— SIN IS SERIOUS, BUT CHRIST IS ENOUGH— IS THE ENEMY'S WORST NIGHTMARE.

#CRASHTHECHATTERBOX

9

Counterfeit Conviction

Perfectionism is the voice of the oppressor.

—ANNE LAMOTT

Have you ever heard of Harold Staley? Well, it's high time you did. Not only was he my boyhood guitar teacher, but he's also the former front man of the Imitation Temptations. That might not mean much to you, but in Moncks Corner, South Carolina, where I grew up, the ITs were it.

At least that's how it seemed to an eight-year-old like me.

And why wouldn't everybody feel the same way? Each Fourth of July they rocked the Moncks Corner Street Dance at the old train depot like it was Wembley Arena.

They wore fancy white tuxedos with tails, and it seemed like a magic trick to me every time Harold hit the high note on "Papa Was a Rolling Stone." ("When he *di-i-i-i-i-ied,* all he left us was a-lo-oh-one.")

Plus, they were backed by Gene, Jack, Donny, and Truman—the Customs 4.

Every little boy needs real-life superheroes—and the Imitation Temptations were mine.

So you can imagine how completely crushed I was when Harold finally explained to me why they were called the *Imitation* Temptations. Since Moncks Corner is more than eight hundred miles from Motown, I never had any reason to suspect that my musical heroes were a cheap knockoff of a *real* group from a million years ago. Learning this was traumatizing, like when you first find out about Santa Claus or Donald Trump's hair.

Of course, growing up means finding out that much of what you thought was real is not. A lot of things you thought were awesome aren't so much. You learn to test for authenticity because survival in adulthood requires it.

Likewise, maturity in Christ is largely about becoming familiar enough with what is true to see through what's false.

Here's how the writer of Hebrews explains what it means to be established in faith:

> Solid food is for the mature, who by constant use have trained themselves to distinguish good from evil. (5:14)

The problem is, most believers never mature enough in their faith to distinguish between conviction and condemnation, good and evil.

Condemnation's greatest talent is *imitation*. Conviction is the work of the Holy Spirit. Condemnation is the Enemy's best impersonation of the Holy Spirit's work. And the chatterbox is as adept at trying to sound like the Holy Spirit as Harold Staley and the boys were at nailing the chime harmonies of "My Girl."

I like the way Jerry Bridges describes it in his book *The Pursuit of Holiness*: "The Holy Spirit makes us more aware of our lack of holiness to stimulate us to deeper yearning and striving for holiness. But Satan will attempt to use the Holy Spirit's work to discourage us."[1]

In an earlier chapter about fear, we began to explore the contrast between the Enemy's threats and God's whispers. In fact, throughout the book we've been drawing an extended contrast. By learning to distinguish between the way God speaks and the way the Enemy speaks, we move toward words of life and grow in the ways of God. Now I want to continue that contrast, digging a little deeper into how this applies specifically to condemnation.

The Three Little *P*'s

I have a friend named Henry Cloud, who is a well-known Christian psychologist. Recently he was at our church, teaching a seminar based on his book *Boundaries for Leaders*. Toward the end of his last session, he started explaining something called "learned helplessness" and the three *p*'s of negative thinking. I was captivated because so much of what he was sharing coalesced with what I've been learning about the chatterbox.

Henry explains in his book how chronic, ongoing failure causes "'software' changes in the brain, and negativity seeps in. And when you have negative expectations, a different chemical cocktail gets brewed in your brain. The result is not just a temporary sense of feeling like 'life sucks,' but a fundamental change in outlook and how experiences get processed."[2]

That's good stuff—but it was the three *p*'s that really got my attention. Citing a study by researcher Martin Seligman, Cloud categorizes negative thinking styles using the following three descriptors:

1. Personal
2. Permanent
3. Pervasive[3]

I want to spend the rest of this chapter talking in depth about those three words.

The Scriptures suggest that children are a gift from the Lord. I affirm this, because where else would I get new material for sermon illustrations every week? I've learned to observe my children closely. Who knows when they'll say or do the perfect thing at the perfect moment that illustrates a future subject I'm preaching or writing about?

Like just now. I opened my laptop to start writing about these three *p*'s. On the other side of the yard, I noticed that Holly had just set up a cornhole board we borrowed. Then I noticed that Elijah was mindlessly jumping on the board. The next thing I know, Holly is reprimanding him, with appropriately mild severity, while folding up the now-broken, inoperative cornhole board.

I silently debated whether to jump in and offer my disciplinary assistance. But I quickly realized it wouldn't be necessary. Elijah was soon apologizing for his actions through tears.

Then I spoke up: "It's okay, buddy. We forgive you. But you will be helping us pay for a new one. That will help you be more careful with others' stuff."

He agreed to chip in, as if it were a suggestion, apologized some more, and then walked away to continue sulking. But what he said under his breath next is the reason I'm telling you about this: "What's *wrong* with me? I *always* mess up *everything!*"

In two short sentences my son had just outlined the three *p*'s of condemnation with a simple profundity that was well worth the cost of the damaged cornhole board.

The three *p*'s of condemnation—from the lips of an eight-year-old. I hope this doesn't feel too elementary, but I'm going to break down his statement. I'm guessing something he said will remind you of your own condemning chatterbox.

PERSONAL: *"What's wrong with ME?"*

He didn't say, "I need to calm down a little and be more careful and responsible."

Instead, he turned it into a reflection of his deep-seated inadequacy. "I broke the board; therefore, something is fundamentally wrong with me. I'll probably end up living in a trash dump with Wreck-It Ralph."

PERMANENT: *"I ALWAYS…"*

Not "Stuff that I stomp on seems to have about a 70 percent casualty rate. So from now on I won't assume every item I see is a dance floor in disguise."

Rather, he's tattooing a new motto on his forehead: "I break stuff…*all the time…all the time…*I break stuff."

PERVASIVE: *"…mess up EVERYTHING!"*

He didn't focus on the issue at hand—his rambunctious disregard for personal property.

Nope. He identified himself as the source of all human unhappiness. (Well, at least next time you see *everything* messed up, you'll know who to blame.)

I'm well aware that the boy was likely turning up the drama in an effort to minimize his consequences. And that he is simply fulfilling one of his purposes on earth by destroying things, thereby helping me more fully appreciate the patience and sacrifice of my own parents. I suppose I should thank him for the added perspective.

But don't you find yourself often entertaining these same types of personal, permanent, pervasive thoughts about your failures and mistakes?

I'm such a…

I always…

I never…

Now everything is…

If we're going to grow in Christ, we can't keep thinking and speaking like little children. Maturing in Christ means developing the ability to decode the Spirit's conviction even as condemnation fills the airwaves of our minds with chatter. It means getting beneath our sweeping feelings of shame, applying the mercy of God to our weakness, and moving forward in greater strength.

So let's consider each of these individual characteristics. How, specifically, do they relate to condemnation?

The three *p*'s are a concise and insightful analysis of the general nature of negative thinking, for sure. But they also provide us with a precise framework for detecting condemnation in our lives. And the better we get at recognizing condemnation, the more confidently we can root it out. Then God can replace it with something *true*.

Later, imitator.

What's Wrong with *Me*?

Condemnation will always prompt you to speak in the first person about your failures and flaws. To a degree, this is appropriate, even helpful.

In the previous chapter we established our responsibility to take our sin seriously. We'll never cure condemnation by blowing off the internal warning signs when something in our hearts isn't right. We'll only give the Accuser more ammunition.

Furthermore, in many respects, God expects us to take our sin *personally*. Blaming other people or circumstances for our actions can be even more destructive than blowing them off. Jesus said to take the log out of our own eyes before pointing out a speck in someone else's.[4] I say that we need to put down the magnifying glass, with which we so thoroughly evaluate the faults of others, and pick up a mirror. Michael Jackson would have agreed—when something needs to change, the best place to start looking for a solution is within. Take a look at yourself.

So, obviously it's necessary—and profitable—to own up to our dysfunctions.

The problem comes when we go beyond confessing our sin (which means agreeing with God about it) and begin defining ourselves according to the sin. In this way we allow our lives to be defined by what we *did* rather than anticipating our tomorrows according to what Christ has done. We allow the Enemy to rob us of the value of grace's great exchange, which is the central proposition of Christianity. We stop learning from our mistakes under the tutelage of the Spirit. And we start accepting labels created by the lies of condemnation.

In her book *Unglued,* my friend Lysa TerKeurst writes about the limitation of living with the wrong kinds of labels. She explains how labels "imprison us in categories that are hard to escape":

> I should know. While I've never been a numbered inmate in a federal prison, I've put labels on myself that have certainly locked me into hard places....
>
> *I am angry.*
> *I am frustrated.*
> *I am a screamer.*
> *I am a stuffer.*
> *I am just like my mother.*
> *I am a wreck.*
> *I am a people pleaser.*
> *I am a jerk.*
> *I am insecure.*
> *I am unglued...*
>
> Those labels start out as little threads of self-dissatisfaction but ultimately weave together into a straightjacket of self-condemnation.[5]

What labels have you been allowing condemnation to slap on you lately? Wouldn't it be nice to start peeling them off and hand the label maker back to God? After all, isn't the manufacturer and owner of an object the only one who has the right to label it? And doesn't God occupy both of those roles in our lives?

You see, if *I* is the most common word in the chatterbox's vocabulary, *God* is the most conspicuously absent. When we stop identifying primarily with our new life in Christ, our performance becomes a self-fulfilling prophecy, with condemnation calling the shots.

Our sin is our personal responsibility, but in Christ it is no longer the center of our identity.

I can't improve on this synopsis by Swiss psychiatrist Carl Jung: "We cannot change anything until we accept it. Condemnation does not liberate, it oppresses."

Freedom is not to be found in denial; neither is freedom to be found in deprecation. It is only to be gained by embracing the paradox of the Cross.

It is a paradox the apostle Paul summarized brilliantly in one of the best-loved verses in the New Testament:

> I have been crucified with Christ and I no longer live, but Christ lives in
> me. The life I now live in the body, I live by faith in the Son of God, who
> loved me and gave himself for me. (Galatians 2:20)

This is the same Paul who said the following about himself in a letter to his protégé Timothy:

> Here is a trustworthy saying that deserves full acceptance: Christ
> Jesus came into the world to save sinners—of whom I am the worst.
> (1 Timothy 1:15)

How can the same man deem himself the "worst of sinners" and yet so confidently claim full association with Christ? The key is in the phrase "Christ... in me."

Yes, this seems to be a contradiction. But there is a difference between a contradiction and a paradox. A contradiction *cannot* be true. A paradox *appears* as if it cannot be true, but something beneath the surface makes it so.

The Christian life is a perpetual paradox. I am crucified, yet I live. I have sinned and continue to sin, yet I am without blame. Not because of the good in me, but because of Christ in me.

In the paradox of my failed performance and God's faithful promise, Christ is revealed. The more He is revealed, the more I become like Him.

So I acknowledge what I was, but I place greater weight on what Christ did to change who I am. And I am being conformed to His image in the process.

None of this excuses me from the responsibility to change. But it liberates me from the bondage of lies so that change is actually possible.

I always...

First person is the default voice of condemnation. But identifying the tense condemnation speaks in is a little trickier because the voice of the Enemy traverses all tenses. He loves to project the past into the future, thus squeezing out the potential of the present.

In other words, condemnation creates hopelessness by convincing you that change is unlikely or impossible. Condemnation interrogates in rooms without windows, making you feel as though you'll never see another sunrise.

In contrast, every time God calls out a deficiency in your life, you can be assured that He is simultaneously offering an invitation. He Himself will fill the voids He is identifying—if you will cooperate. I could provide pages of examples of these kinds of invitations, but this one is my favorite. In these verses the prophet Isaiah is pleading with rebellious Israel on God's behalf:

> Come, all you who are thirsty,
>   come to the waters;
> and you who have no money,
>   come, buy and eat!
> Come, buy wine and milk
>   without money and without cost.
> Why spend money on what is not bread,
>   and your labor on what does not satisfy?
> Listen, listen to me, and eat what is good,
>   and you will delight in the richest of fare. (Isaiah 55:1–2)

The book of Isaiah delivers oracle after oracle of impending punishment for the people's repeated violation of their covenant with God. Yet, in the final section of his prophecy, Isaiah sounds the first notes of the invitation hymn: "Come."

That's God's favorite way to start conversations with His children: "Come."

By contrast, condemnation will never call you to come into God's presence. It will convince you that you have nowhere to go because of where you've been. One of my friends told me that the most prominent feature of depression is the unremitting belief that things will never get any better than they are right now. In the same way, one of the most prominent features of condemnation is the unshakable sensation that I'll never change from who I am right now. I've always struggled with this; therefore, I'll never conquer it.

Condemnation is the older brother in the parable of the prodigal son. He wrongly believes—and wants to make you believe—that because you went to the pigpen, the pigpen should be your permanent mailing address.

But it's not his house we're returning to or his rules we're abiding by. The Father makes a different proclamation:

This son of mine *was* dead and *is* alive again; he *was* lost and *is* found. (Luke 15:24, emphasis added)

Now that's more like it. The past is buried (he *was* dead); the present is resurrected (he *is* alive). That's the way the Father speaks. He understands the correct usage of tenses. What *was* does not determine what *will be,* because God is in every moment, redeeming it for His glory.

And it gets even better than that. Not only does the Spirit set us free from chains that have bound us to our past, but He actually unleashes the Father's vision of our future into our present reality.

That's why Jesus could say about Peter, "I tell you that you are Peter, and on this rock I will build my church, and the gates of Hades will not overcome it," only to directly correct and confront Peter just verses later: "Get behind me, Satan! You are a stumbling block to me; you do not have in mind the concerns of God, but merely human concerns" (Matthew 16:18, 23).

Peter was completely missing the point of why Jesus came to earth. His priorities were in the wrong place, and Jesus called him something much worse than a silly goose for it. Peter would later deny even knowing Jesus at the most crucial moment of His life and ministry.

But Peter's present mind-set and performance weren't the biggest determining factors in his potential for building God's kingdom. Jesus, who knows all things, already knew Peter was about to act as a stumbling block at the same time He was calling him a solid rock.

He called him a rock anyway.

See, God's assessment of you isn't limited by where you've been *before* or even where you are *now.* His words reflect the places He plans to take you and the purposes He intends to fulfill through you.

A couple of years ago I made my first trip to Australia. When I landed, after nineteen hours of flying, I decided to FaceTime the family back home. I wanted to show the kids what Australia looks like and see them before they went to bed. It was about 10:00 a.m. on Wednesday in Sydney, which meant it was 8:00 p.m. on Tuesday in Charlotte.

I did my best to show the kids a few of the sights through the hotel window. They were disappointed by the absence of kangaroos. And confused by one other thing.

"Daddy," Elijah asked, "why is it daytime there?"

I tried to explain to the kids about Australia being in a different hemisphere and how it's across the International Date Line.

"Basically," I summarized, "it's tomorrow here."

Judging by the response, I was sure my geography lesson had sailed right over their heads. Then at the end of the conversation as we were about to have our prayer and say goodnight, Elijah let me know otherwise. "Daddy, before you go, can you tell us what happens tomorrow?"

Let me tell you, it's a pretty powerful feeling to deliver messages from the future.

"Tomorrow," I started, "is an awesome day. Tomorrow you have perfect behavior. Tomorrow you get along. Tomorrow you respect your Mommy…"

I swear I saw Holly trying to give me an offering through the computer.

What I was pretending to do in that moment, God actually has the ability to do—every day of our lives. The One who lives outside of time invites you into a reality that is informed by His perfect plans to give you hope and a future.

God speaks in the past tense about battles you're currently fighting.

And He buries the shame of yesterday in order to resurrect the moment you are in and sustain you in the season He is calling you to embrace.

Judas went out and hanged himself following his betrayal of Jesus, unable to imagine a redemptive end to his story.

After denying Jesus, Peter went on to preach on the day of Pentecost and help establish the Jerusalem church.

One was led by the voice of condemnation, which insisted his failure was permanent: *You'll always be a traitor.*

The other had experienced the power of conviction and the tenderness of compassion by receiving the words of Christ: *On this rock I will build my church, and the gates of Hades* will not *overcome it.*

What are the words of Christ for you and me, then? I would offer these: *You'll* always *be chosen. Nothing can stop God's work in your life.*

Condemnation will construct gallows out of your flaws and failures. But the Spirit's conviction will point you to the Cross, where the cost of those sins has already been satisfied. And the Father's compassion will fill you with forgiveness, raising you to new life...

Over and over again.

...mess up everything!

Have you seen any of those commercials about all the terrible things that will happen if you don't switch to DirecTV? I'm sure it won't be nearly as funny this way, but here's a transcript of my favorite one:

When your cable company keeps you on hold, you get angry.

When you get angry, you go blow off steam.

When you go blow off steam, accidents happen.

When accidents happen, you get an eye patch.

When you get an eye patch, people think you're tough.

When people think you're tough, people want to see how tough.

When people want to see how tough, you end up in a roadside ditch.

Don't wake up in a roadside ditch.

Get rid of cable and upgrade to DirecTV.

This is my kind of humor—the more over the top, the better. Most people who know me would probably say that I'm pretty over the top—all or nothing—in almost every area of my life. In so many ways this works for me. It makes me passionate and driven and obsessive about some things that really matter, like my family, my ministry, and my walk with God.

But as Oswald Chambers said, "Unguarded strength is double weakness."[6] And the same all-or-nothing mentality that can be a powerful tool when submitted to the Spirit can be a deadly weapon in the hands of condemnation.

For instance, when discipline in one area of my life starts to slide, it spreads quickly to all the other areas and gets blown way out of proportion:

When I miss exercising three weeks in a row, my pants start to feel a little tight.

When my pants start to feel a little tight, I snooze the alarm a few extra times because I dread going through the exercise of finding pants that fit.

When I hit the snooze button on my alarm clock too many times, I get a week behind on my YouVersion Bible reading plan.

When I get a week behind on my YouVersion Bible reading plan, I'm embarrassed to pray because I feel like I'm delinquent in my commitment to God.

When I'm not praying very much, I start behaving manipulatively and carnally, creating situations that could have been avoided.

If only I'd switched to DirecTV.

I mean, stayed consistent with my exercise regimen.

Maybe the dominoes fall in a different sequence for you. What sets you off may be completely unrelated to the things I just mentioned. But I'm sure you've experienced the hell ride I'm describing: making a few small missteps, waking up in a ditch, pulling at your eye patch, wondering what happened.

That's because condemnation is *pervasive*. It is not satisfied to wreck one room in your life; it wants to cut the gas line, light a match, and watch the whole thing burn.

There are two ways to stop this from happening.

The first is never ever screw up. Never. Never miss a day at the gym, a morning devotion, a Sunday at church, an opportunity to serve or encourage, a dentist appointment, or a donation to the volunteer fire department. Never lust, never envy, never gossip, never try tobacco or processed foods—and pray without ceasing for the peace of Jerusalem.

If you can live this way flawlessly, congratulations! Your perfection will starve condemnation to death. This is, by the way, what Paul said the law was powerless to do—because it was weakened by the flesh.

In other words, it's a bad plan. It can't be done.

Thank God for Jesus. Because He came, a better way is available.

Let's look at Romans 8:3 again, but this time let's read it in context:

What the law was powerless to do because it was weakened by the
flesh, God did by sending his own Son in the likeness of sinful flesh
to be a sin offering. And so he condemned sin in the flesh, in order

that the righteous requirement of the law might be fully met in us,
who do not live according to the flesh but according to the Spirit.
(Romans 8:3–4)

The truth in that passage is forceful enough to pull up condemnation by its roots.

Read the passage again. Digest it. Own it. Declare it. Read it again.

Most of all, notice the key contrast: what *I* could never do, *God already did!*

As a believer, I no longer live under the tyranny of condemnation, because God, the righteous Judge, condemned my sin in Christ. *ALL. All* of it!

Now the Spirit of God has shut the mouth of condemnation, rendering it mute when it comes face to face with all who are in Christ, for all eternity.

And this power is activated with this simple confession:

God says He has.

God Flipped It

Here's a little story for you to recall the next time the Accuser starts his stuff with you. I bet I've shared this story over three hundred times in churches all over the world. I'm pretty sure it's fictional. But it brings down the house every time.

There was an elderly lady who stood up one Sunday night during a testimony service in her little church and grabbed the mic. She said, "I just want to tell everybody how good God has been to me. You see, I was down to my last twenty dollars, and I gave it in the offering last week. I didn't really know where my next meal was going to come from, my cupboards were empty, but I gave anyway and went home trusting God, hallelujah!"

She explained how her neighbor was an atheist and how he took every opportunity to mock her faith. "How can you trust in God," he would prod, "when He's done such a poor job providing for you?"

So when he heard she'd given her last twenty dollars, the neighbor decided to have a little fun with the old woman. He went to the store, purchased several bags of groceries, crept over to her house while she was inside, and placed the groceries on her front step. Then he knocked three times on the door and ran off to hide on his porch, awaiting her reaction.

Well, when the woman came out and saw the groceries, she got *happy*. All she could say was, "God did it! God did it! God did it!"

She said this over and over again, getting louder and louder each time. Her slow pacing on the front porch was slowly evolving into a full-blown dance, and now she was shouting: "God did it! God did it! God did it!"

Finally the atheist could stand no more. He sprinted to the steps of the woman's porch and shouted, "Gotcha!"

Not knowing, or really caring, what he was talking about, the lady repeated, "God did it!"

"*God* didn't do it," the neighbor objected. "*I* bought the groceries."

Unfazed, she replied, "God did it! God did it! God *did* it!"

Exasperated, the atheist screamed, "God didn't do *anything*! Because your God doesn't exist! Here's the receipt for the groceries. *I* bought them so you'd finally be forced to admit that God is a figment of your imagination!"

After a long pause the woman declared, "*God* did it, and he made the devil *pay* for it!"

The next time the Enemy starts bombarding your mind with condemnation— about events that happened seconds ago or decades ago—make him pay. Take the opportunity to remind him of what God did and what He has promised to do for you.

God says He has saved me. And He is saving me.

God says He has forgiven me. And His grace is cleansing me.

God says He has called me. And His mercy is keeping me.

God says He has rescued my life from the pit. And His kindness is crowning me with love and compassion.

I promise you, the chatterbox can't stand very much of this. Rehearsing the gospel—the good news of what Christ has done—will set off a nuclear melt-down in condemnation's generating station.

Make the devil pay by reminding him of what Christ has done to redeem your past.

Renew your hope and confidence by reminding yourself of what Christ has done to secure your future.

Flip the script on the chatterbox.

Instead of allowing condemnation to make failure *personal*—labeling you with guilt and shame—allow God to personalize in your heart the love He has already demonstrated on the cross. *God so loved, not just the world as a whole but me as a person, that He gave His only Son.*

Instead of cementing yourself in past and current struggles and failures, affirm the *permanence* of the love of Christ. This love is the *only* thing that correctly claims to last forever. *I am convinced that nothing—in all creation—will ever be able to separate me from the love of God in Christ Jesus my Lord.*

And when the chatter starts in one area, don't allow it access to every part of your life. Instead, allow your mind to be *pervaded* with an awareness of the fullness of Him who fills all things everywhere and yet still chooses to dwell in the brokenness of our hearts.

For most of us, none of this is new information. We already know plenty about what Christ has done.

But there's a vast difference between knowing *about* what He's done and *knowing it*. Knowing *about* it informs your mind. *Knowing* it—personally—will transform your heart and illuminate your path.

In fact, as we're about to see, what we call spiritual progress is usually not about something we need to learn.

It's about something we need to *remember*.

GOD SPEAKS IN THE PAST TENSE
ABOUT BATTLES YOU'RE
CURRENTLY FIGHTING.

#CRASHTHECHATTERBOX

10

The Divine Reminder

Memory can make a thing seem to have been much more than it was.

—MARILYNNE ROBINSON, *GILEAD*

I meet with a professional Christian counselor about once a month—and if you've made it this far in the book, I'm sure you don't need any more examples of why I need his services. In all seriousness, I meet with Lance because I need someone to help me process my own chatter. There is something about verbally expressing your internal struggles that objectifies them. And it's good to know that the person I'm expressing my struggles to is obligated not to express them to anyone else.

Lance has walked with me through a lot of battles and dilemmas, and I greatly value his insights. But one day as I was going on and on about something I was working through, I had an insight of my own.

"Lance, I just figured out something," I said, smiling.

He just looked at me the way counselors do, with the classic tell-me-more look, which kind of proved the point I was about to make.

I continued. "I mean, I like you. I love you. But you don't ever really tell me anything I don't already know."

He leaned forward and said, "Tell me more about that."

"See, that's what I'm talking about! All you do is keep me talking until I remember what I already know and say what I need to hear. You should be writing me a check after every session for all this incredible advice you get to hear me give to myself."

We were both laughing, and I was thinking about something Jesus said about the Holy Spirit. In John 14:26, Jesus called the Holy Spirit "the Counselor." Now most translations render the word "Advocate" or "Helper." But in the translation I memorized, the word is "Counselor," and that's what came to my mind while I was talking to Lance.

Here's the full verse in the very words of Jesus:

> The Counselor, the Holy Spirit, whom the Father will send in my name, will teach you all things and will remind you of everything I have said to you. (John 14:26, NIV 1984)

The Scriptures mention more than seventy different functions of the Holy Spirit. In the last couple of chapters, we've discussed one of those functions in depth: how Jesus sent the Holy Spirit to convict us of our sin. He explained to His disciples:

> I tell you the truth: It is for your good that I am going away. Unless I go away, the Counselor will not come to you; but if I go, I will send him to you. When he comes, he will convict the world of guilt in regard to sin and righteousness and judgment. (John 16:7–8, NIV 1984)

We've talked at length about the difference between conviction and condemnation. But so far we've approached it mostly from the standpoint of how to recognize the voice of condemnation. In other words, our focus has been on training our ears to hear what the negative chatter sounds like.

However, I've heard that the best way to learn to spot a counterfeit is to become intimately familiar with the real thing.

So what does the real thing—the voice of the Holy Spirit—sound like? We've seen how condemnation works, but how exactly does conviction operate in the life of a believer? In this chapter I want to talk about one of the seventy functions of the Holy Spirit that is, to me, one of the most overlooked yet all-important functions of the Spirit in the life of every believer. Without it, we'll never access the fullness of the Spirit's power.

I want us to consider how the Holy Spirit—the Counselor—is our *Divine Reminder*.

Because the fact is, most of us are already educated far beyond the level of our obedience. We need God's help to remember—and obey—the revelation we already have.

The Life You Forget

I love this opening section of Donald Miller's book *A Million Miles in a Thousand Years:*

> The saddest thing about life is *you don't remember half of it.* You don't
> even remember half of half of it. Not even a tiny percentage, if you want
> to know the truth. I have this friend Bob who writes down everything he
> remembers. If he remembers dropping an ice cream cone on his lap when
> he was seven, he'll write it down. The last time I talked to Bob, he had
> written more than five hundred pages of memories. He's the only guy I
> know who remembers his life. He said he captures memories, because if
> he forgets them, it's as though they didn't happen; *it's as though he hadn't*
> *lived the parts he doesn't remember.*[1]

If you think about it, not only is it remarkable how much of life we *don't* remember; it's bizarre what we *do* remember—and what we forget. For example, most people would have a hard time telling me the passage the pastor preached on last time they were in church.

But if I say the words "In West Philadelphia born and raised," every single American reader born between 1975 and 1983 will automatically respond, with a catechized precision, "On the playground was where I spent most of my days." And without assistance they could continue reciting—word for word—the entire theme song from *The Fresh Prince of Bel-Air.*

I don't mean this as a rebuke, although a Jesus Juke would be most fitting right about now: "Y'all have more passion for Carlton than you do for Christ… oh, smack."

I'm just saying, it's crazy what we tend to remember and what we tend to forget. Our human memories, even as believers, are incredibly *selective.* And it's not even like we're the ones making the selections much of the time.

The Counselor and the chatterbox both have the same goal—to remind us. It's what they're reminding us *of* that sets them apart.

This has much deeper implications than the theme song of an early nineties sitcom. The chatterbox wants us to forget what God wants us to remember, while it reminds us of what God wants us to forget.

That's where the Counselor comes in. While the chatterbox reminds us of our wrongs by showing us our shame over and over again, the Spirit convicts us of our sin by reminding us of our righteousness.

The Look

In the last chapter we talked about how Peter's failure was not final because of the better word Jesus spoke over his future. We looked at what Jesus said to Peter before the failure and how God's grace restored Peter following the failure.

But, personally, I think one of the most poignant parts of Peter's story happened in the exact *moment* when he came face to face with his failure. It comes just after the third time Peter had denied Jesus—the very thing he had insisted he would never do.

> Just as he was speaking, the rooster crowed. The Lord turned and looked straight at Peter. *Then Peter remembered* the word the Lord had spoken to him: "Before the rooster crows today, you will disown me three times."
> And he went outside and wept bitterly. (Luke 22:60–62, emphasis added)

I sense a haunting quality in the phrase "Then Peter remembered..." Do you?

Not only does Peter remember Jesus's prediction about the failure of his faith. You have to assume that he also remembers the bravado and boldness with which he had denied the possibility that this could *ever* happen to someone as committed as he.[2]

"*Never, Lord! I'll* never *deny you! They might...but I* never *will!*"

Suddenly a single sound—*Cock-a-doodle-doo!*—jars Peter from a state of disillusionment and denial, pulling him to the depths of remorse, contrition, and humiliation. It's deep enough to bring him to his breaking point: "And he went outside and wept bitterly."

How many memories Peter must have had in that moment and in the days that would follow. I'll bet he remembered much more than the warning of Jesus in the upper room.

In a flood of flashbacks, maybe he remembers how the voice of Jesus had called him to *come* on the storm-tossed Sea of Galilee late one night. And how,

moments after he'd placed the ball of his foot onto the uncertainty of water and
had begun to sink, Jesus had reached out and saved him. Perhaps he remembered the walk he took with Jesus back to the boat. Maybe he and Jesus shared
a private conversation in that moment that wasn't meant to be recorded. I'm sure
they had many of these kinds of moments. I suspect some of them came back to
Peter, and he saw them in his mind's eye…with the soundtrack of the rooster's
crow.

Whatever he does or doesn't remember, certainly he remembers the confident endorsement of Jesus: "I tell you that you are Peter, and on this rock I will
build my church, and the gates of Hades will not overcome it."[3]

But now it appears the gates of hell have prevailed—against Peter at least.
The rooster has crowed, the test is over, and Peter has disappointed the One he
had pledged his life to serve.

And it was the crow of the rooster that reminded Peter and brought him to
a point of repentance.

Or was it?

Let's look at the verse again, more carefully this time:

Just as he was speaking, the rooster crowed. The Lord turned and looked
straight at Peter. *Then* Peter remembered…

It may seem like a small detail, but it contains a meaningful revelation: Peter
wasn't reminded of the word Jesus had spoken by the crow of the rooster. He was
reminded by the *look* of the Lord.

How do you think Jesus looked at Peter in that moment?

Do you think He revealed an expression of disappointment? That's impossible. How could the One who foretold this very incident be disappointed by its
occurrence?

Or do you think Jesus put on His angry eyes before He fixed his gaze on
Peter? I doubt it, considering Jesus had plans to invite this guy to be the guest
speaker on the day of Pentecost.

I'm sure there was a measure of hurt and sadness in the Savior's eyes. But
mostly I think that when the Lord looked at Peter, Peter saw the same thing he'd
always seen in the countenance of the man who had inspired his total allegiance
for the last three years.

I believe Jesus looked at Peter with a look of love. And it was not the crow of condemnation but the look of the Lord's love that brought Peter to a place of repentance.

You may think I'm making too much of a small biblical detail. I get it—I'm inferring a lot. But isn't this consistent with the truth we've been studying so far in the Scriptures? Isn't it the kindness of the Lord that leads us to repentance?

Haven't we seen that the Spirit convicts believers of sin, not by rubbing our noses in our mistakes (we already know these too well), but by reminding us of our righteousness in Christ? He brings to our attention the incredible realities of salvation that our defective memories seem to frequently forget.

But when we look into the face of Christ, we *remember*.

Here Comes the Rooster

It hit me recently that many believers suffer the effects of spiritual face blindness. You've heard of face blindness, haven't you? I saw a fascinating news report about it recently. People who have this disorder can see ordinary objects all around them, so there's nothing wrong with their actual eyesight. They simply can't *recognize* faces—even those of people they've known their whole lives, like their moms, their dads, their sons, their daughters, or their spouses. How difficult to go through life seeing the form of the faces of those you love but not being able to correctly perceive their identities.

The crow of condemnation wants to divert your attention and erase your spiritual memory so that you aren't able to behold the face of Christ. *Cock-a-doodle-doo! You're a loser. You're worthless. You're inconsistent.*

But remember, if the rooster is crowing, that means it's morning. And that means the sun is coming up again.

In the Spirit of God, we have a light that reveals to us who God is, what He is like, and what He desires to do in our lives. Paul puts it this way in 2 Corinthians 4:6:

> God, who said, "Let light shine out of darkness," made his light shine in
> our hearts to give us the light of the knowledge of God's glory displayed
> in the face of Christ.

Jesus puts the same light that was active in creation in our hearts by giving us His Spirit to gently remind us of what we already know. The Counselor reaffirms the Father's love for us in our moments of failure by showing us the face of Christ.

But the Spirit's conviction sounds nothing like condemnation's *cock-a-doodle-doo*. It looks like the face of Jesus. And this face is radiant with love and compassion.

Remember to Forget

I'm sure Peter heard many more roosters crowing throughout the duration of his life. I have visited the Galilean countryside, and even today it is nearly impossible to avoid—or ignore—the sound.

Yet when Peter wrote his letter to the Jerusalem church, over thirty years after his epic failure in the courtyard, here's what he had to say about the value of spiritual memory:

> My brothers, be all the more eager to make your calling and election *sure*. For if you do these things, you will *never fall*, and you will receive a rich welcome into the eternal kingdom of our Lord and Savior Jesus Christ.
>
> So *I will always remind you* of these things, even though you know them and are firmly established in the truth you now have. I think it is right to *refresh your memory* as long as I live in the tent of this body, because I know that I will soon put it aside, as our Lord Jesus Christ has made clear to me. And I will make every effort to see that after my departure you will *always be able to remember* these things. (2 Peter 1:10–15, NIV 1984, emphasis added)

Look at that first paragraph again. Make your calling *sure*? *Never* fall? How could the man who failed so miserably—and publicly—make such a promise? How is the disciple whose uncertainty made him sink to the bottom like a rock now giving instructions on how to be *sure*?

Peter had been changed by the power of the Holy Spirit. The pain and paralysis of what he did has been displaced by the constant memory of what Christ has done. And now he writes to refresh the memories of believers so that they may be established in the truth and be set free from the chains of condemnation.

The philosopher George Santayana famously said, "Those who cannot remember the past are condemned to repeat it."[4] The gospel, however, says that those who do not *forget* the past are condemned to repeat it.

By looking to the Lord and beholding His love for us, we not only remember His benefits, mercies, and provision. We are also enabled to forget our shame, our sin, and our shortcomings.

It seems strange to say, but in order to complete the change, the same Spirit who labors to help us remember must also make us forget. Here are two of my favorite scriptures—one from the Old Testament and one from the New Testament—that emphasize the biblical importance of forgetting.

> This is what the LORD says—
>   he who made a way through the sea,
>   a path through the mighty waters,
> who drew out the chariots and horses,
>   the army and reinforcements together,
> and they lay there, never to rise again,
>   extinguished, snuffed out like a wick:
> "*Forget the former things;*
>   *do not dwell on the past.*
> See, I am doing a new thing!
>   Now it springs up; do you not perceive it?
> I am making a way in the wilderness
>   and streams in the wasteland." (Isaiah 43:16–19, emphasis added)

> Brothers, I do not consider myself yet to have taken hold of it. But one thing I do: *Forgetting what is behind* and straining toward what is ahead, I press on toward the goal to win the prize for which God has called me heavenward in Christ Jesus. (Philippians 3:13–14, NIV 1984, emphasis added)

I don't interpret the call to Spirit-led forgetfulness to mean that it's possible for me to no longer be *conscious* of the wrong things I've done. Rather, it means I will no longer be *controlled* by those wrongs.

It is the active memory of God's faithfulness to me and Christ's sacrifice for me that makes me able to forget.

The Hidden Hymn Book

My grandmother died of Alzheimer's disease over a decade ago. At first the effects of her disease were subtle. "Steven, how's school?" she'd ask, only to repeat the question a dozen more times over the course of a three-hour visit. But this was just the beginning of a deterioration that was agonizing to watch. I can't imagine what it was like for her to go through it.

Toward the end of her life, after twelve years of suffering, the disease had pretty much erased the hard drive of her memory. She couldn't remember who I was or who my mom—her daughter—was. She couldn't even remember the name of her husband of more than fifty years, although he stayed at her side daily, combing her hair, telling her how beautiful she was, until the very end.

Most tragically of all, perhaps, I don't think she remembered who *she* was as her life came to a close. Most of her waking hours were spent either in catatonic confusion or sheer terror. It was incomprehensible to me why, at the end of her life, the Lord allowed her to lose all the memories that had made her life so remarkable.

In spite of all this, there's one thing she never forgot—and I'll never forget this either. She never forgot how to sing the hymns she had hidden in her heart.

My grandfather had been a Methodist minister all his adult life. And his wife had been by his side, on the front row, at every church he ever served. She had been fully present, praying the prayers, hearing the sermons, and singing the hymns every Sunday, week after week, decade after decade.

So when we'd go sit with Grandma at the nursing home and try to start a conversation, nothing would happen. But when we'd start singing something like "Great is Thy faithfulness, O God my Father," she'd pick up the next line: "There is no shadow of turning with Thee." And she'd continue on, singing verses I'd never even heard before, remembering almost every word.

It made an incredible impression on me. I was amazed how her weakened voice would recall the notes and the syllables that had shaped her throughout her whole life. And for a few moments during those visits, we almost forgot her sickness as we remembered God in worship together.

She had spent her life allowing the Spirit of God to fill her with eternal truth. And she never forgot it, even when she could remember nothing else.

I never did quiz her on *The Fresh Prince of Bel-Air,* though.

####

When Jesus served the first Communion meal to His disciples—in the same upper room where Peter's failure was foreshadowed—it was a simple commemoration:

He took bread, gave thanks and broke it, and gave it to them, saying, "This is my body given for you; do this *in remembrance of me.*" (Luke 22:19, emphasis added)

Obviously, this is an instruction for a specific ordinance of worship that Jesus instituted. For centuries, churches all over the world have been celebrating the Lord's Supper in honor of Christ's command.

But could it also be an invitation to constant communion with Christ? For each of us, everywhere, each day? And could it be that, in that communion, condemnation is silenced, due to the presence of a compassion that is infinitely greater?

What are the realities of righteousness that God is prompting you to remember right now?

What are the sins in your past that He is urging you to forget?

How long will you allow the rooster to remind you of the words you spoke and can't take back? Or the opportunities you missed?

Instead of being reminded of your past by the Enemy, isn't it time you were reminded of your future by the Lord?

Haven't you spent enough time in the courtyard, dragging your feet to the slow shuffle of condemnation's cadence?

Wouldn't you rather run to the empty tomb and take your stand with the Savior, who has already been in your tomorrow and declared total victory over every area of your life?

Don't you have a hymn in your heart to sing?

CONDEMNATION REMINDS
US OF OUR WRONGS
BY SHOWING US OUR SHAME,
BUT THE SPIRIT CONVICTS US
OF OUR SIN BY REMINDING US
OF OUR RIGHTEOUSNESS IN CHRIST.

#CRASHTHECHATTERBOX

SECTION 4

In which we overpower

the lies of discouragement

with the truth

God says I can.

New level —
New devil :-(

11

Keep Rolling

I'm sick of following my dreams. I'm just going to ask where they're going and hook up with 'em later.

—MITCH HEDBERG

No matter how much we learn about the way chatter works, or how sincerely we commit to doing God's will in spite of the chatter, there's one thing we can count on: the chatter will keep coming. Every day of our lives, for the rest of our lives.

And there's more. It actually gets worse.

The more you grow in Christ and the closer you get to fulfilling the things He put you on the earth to do, the more *intense* the battle with your chatter becomes.

I wish someone had explained this to me a long time ago.

Ever since I became a Christian, I've heard a lot of talk about going to new levels in our relationship with God. Given my competitive nature, that kind of language works for me. When we were naming our church, that was one of the reasons I liked the name Elevation. I loved the idea of helping people take their faith to the next level. I still do. Plus, Elevation was the name of the 2001 U2 world tour, and there is no more certain route to Christian relevance than mimicking whatever U2 did a few years earlier.

Back to what I was saying about levels… Here's the part I didn't get.

I thought going to the next level was mostly about gaining advantages and benefits. I thought, for example, when you got to the next level, you'd have infinite optimism. I thought you'd have total biblical insight. You'd never lack passion or focus or wisdom once you got to the next level.

I thought progressing in God meant you got upgraded equipment to fight the devil, like Link picked up better swords as he advanced through the Overworld in *The Legend of Zelda*.

And in many ways I was right. The more you walk with Christ and fill your mind and heart with His truth, the sharper you become spiritually—more skillful at spiritual warfare, more thoroughly trained in righteousness, more acutely aware of the Spirit's voice.

But here's what they often don't tell you about going higher in God.

At the next level the bosses get bigger and the battles get more complicated. It can seem like the next level is actually designed to keep you out. That's because the resistance is always fiercest on the borderline of a breakthrough.

What can you expect when you start resisting the chatter, pushing past insecurity and fear and condemnation, moving in the direction of the voice of the Lord? Louder chatter, increased resistance, and greater discouragement.

I know this sounds pessimistic and backward, but I can prove that it's true.

Publishing the Struggle

Let's try an experiment. I want you to think of the name of a Christian from the last hundred years who really demonstrated what it means to be like Christ. The person whose name, more than any other in the last century, serves as a household name for humility, love, and the compassion of Jesus.

Got it?

Is the person you thought of…Mother Teresa? And if it wasn't, can we pretend that it was so as not to spoil the illusion of my mental powers or screw up my point?

Few people would argue that Mother Teresa was used by God like few others in the twentieth century. She began her missionary activity in India in 1929. Eventually she formed the organization known as the Missionaries of Charity, which by 2012 consisted of more than 4,500 sisters and was active in 133 countries. Although her legacy has been embattled by controversy, her life stands as an iconic example of the incarnate love and compassion of Christ. Her ministry was marked by acclaim and accomplishment, including a Nobel Peace Prize. And, later, beatification by the pope.

Of course, since she lived in the same horrendous destitution as those she served in Calcutta, her life was also one of intense suffering and poverty.

These are the best-known facts about Mother Teresa. Her highlight reel, you might say.

Who would know better what it means to hear from God and live on a *higher level* in Him than a beatified Nobel Peace Prize winner?

Recently I read some of the entries in *Mother Teresa: Come Be My Light,* a collection of many of her letters, diary notes, and written devotions. A reading of this book makes it clear that she experienced suffering at many levels, not just physical ones. It wasn't just the difficulty of her life in general but also her own doubts and spiritual travail that disheartened her.

You see, even the superior general of the order of the Sisters of Loreto had a behind-the-scenes where the chatter was, at certain points, so overpoweringly discouraging and dark that she doubted everything she had based her life on.

On September 3, 1959, she wrote a letter to Jesus that included the following confessions:

> From my childhood You have called me and kept me for Your own—
> and now when we both have taken the same road—now Jesus—I go the
> wrong way.
>
> They say people in hell suffer eternal pain because of the loss of
> God—they would go through all that suffering if they just had a little
> hope of possessing God.—In my soul I feel just that terrible pain of
> loss—of God not wanting me—of God not being God—of God not
> really existing (Jesus, please forgive my blasphemies—I have been told to
> write everything). That darkness surrounds me on all sides—I can't lift
> my soul to God—no light or inspiration enters my soul.—I speak of love
> for souls—of tender love for God—words pass through my [lips]—and
> I long with a deep longing to believe in them....
>
> I beg of You only one thing—please do not take the trouble to
> return soon.—I am ready to wait for You for all eternity.[1]

It wasn't on just one occasion, or just in her prayer journals, that she spoke this way. In 1957 she wrote the following in a letter to Father Joseph Neuner:

Now Father—since [1949 or 1950] this terrible sense of loss—this untold darkness—this loneliness—this continual longing for God—which gives me that pain down deep in my heart.—Darkness is such that I really do not see—neither with my heart nor with my reason.—The place of God in my soul is blank.—There is no God in me.—When the pain of longing is so great—I just long & long for God—then it is that I feel— He does not want me—He is not there.—Heaven—souls—why these are just words—which mean nothing to me....—My very life seems so contradictory. I help souls—to go where?... —From my childhood I have had a most tender love for Jesus in the Blessed Sacrament—but this too has gone.—I feel nothing before Jesus—and yet I would not miss Holy [Communion] for anything.[2]

The first time I saw these excerpts, I couldn't believe what I was reading—or rather, who had written it. It felt more like I was reading a 3:00 a.m. Kanye West novella-length Twitter confessional than the words of a spiritual hero.

If Mother Teresa, in doing the will of God for her life, never found a way to completely crash the chatterbox, what possible hope do the rest of us have?

Unless—perhaps—we find another way to look at it.

If Mother Teresa never completely crashed the chatterbox yet still found a way to do the will of God for her life, I can do the same.

Read her words again: "I feel nothing before Jesus—*and yet* I would not miss Holy [Communion] for anything."

Some have cited Teresa's dark nights of the soul as proof that her faith was not legitimate. How ironic! I find the fact that she served God while simultaneously dealing with a depression that would have derailed most people an even more convincing proof of her faith than her service itself!

In fact, I wish every spiritual hero were required to publish this kind of journal to Jesus. And they wouldn't be allowed to fill the margins with hearts and flowers or the pages with clichés and rhetoric. They'd actually have to admit the debilitating discouragement that is part of daily life for anyone who does the will of God.

Unfortunately, very few believers, especially publicly revered ones, are willing to risk this level of vulnerability. So the false perception is perpetuated:

*Certain people don't deal with the kind of discouragement I deal with. That's why
God can use them. And that's why He can't use someone like me.*

We don't have nearly enough records of great saints who were willing
to transcribe their actual, unfiltered struggles with doubt, despondency, and
discouragement.

But we do have a few.

Next Level Paradox

In the last chapter we looked at this declaration from the pen of the apostle Paul:

> God, who said, "Let light shine out of darkness," made his light shine in
> our hearts to give us the light of the knowledge of God's glory displayed
> in the face of Christ. (2 Corinthians 4:6)

Now, that's some beautiful imagery. The perfect picture of what it means to
be a believer. No darkness, only light. No confusion and chaos, only the increas-
ing knowledge of God's glory.

Maybe some of the recipients of this letter were shaking their heads a little
at this point: *Yeah, Paul, you're so next level, but what about the rest of us?*

That's why I love the Bible. Because it doesn't only post pictures using filters
of light, knowledge, and glory. It exposes the rest of the story to encourage the
rest of us.

In the verses that follow, Paul dives headfirst into the brokenness and discouragement that were part of his daily experience as a disciple:

> But we have this treasure in jars of clay to show that this all-surpassing
> power is from God and not from us. We are hard pressed on every side,
> but not crushed; perplexed, but not in despair; persecuted, but not
> abandoned; struck down, but not destroyed. We always carry around in
> our body the death of Jesus, so that the life of Jesus may also be revealed
> in our body. (verses 7–10)

Paul isn't interviewing for a consulting gig by presenting a portfolio of all
his next-level accomplishments. He's inviting the people he loves to open their

hearts to the same glory that produces the life of Jesus in him *even in the midst of* persecution, pressure, and death.

It is not a glory that eliminates discouragement.

It is a glory that overcomes discouragement.

It is a glory that runs full speed toward impending opposition with the confidence that, in the collision, Christ will prevail. Even if it doesn't look that way sometimes.

Hold up! you're saying to yourself right now. *I thought you were teaching me how to crash the chatterbox, not how to live under the crushing weight of insecurity, fear, condemnation, and discouragement for the rest of my life. I can do miserable all by myself.*

Is it too late for me to trade in this book for an iTunes gift card?

Remember, Christ is revealed in the paradox: It *is* possible to hear God's voice above all others. But it is also possible to hear all the other voices *above God's.*

The thing is, the chatterbox cannot be crashed once and for all. It has to be dealt with daily.

The people who are called to do great things for God—Mother Teresa, the apostle Paul, and you and me—aren't called to lives where we never have to face discouragement. We must not expect our lives to be so well watered with thoughts of peace, purpose, and power that our souls will never feel dry.

Sorry, but that's not what the next level looks like. Instead, it requires finding a source of strength that runs deeper than circumstances and is not cut off by surges of discouragement.

Going to the next level isn't about graduating from difficult circumstances and dark emotions. It's resolving to live with the mind-set that declares, *My joy is not determined by what happens to me but by what Christ is doing in me and through me.*

Lodge Lockdown

Can I share a page with you from my journal to Jesus? I don't actually keep such a journal, and I'm not Mother Teresa, although I did grow up in a town that was named after the monks at Mepkin Abbey. The fact that I originated from there should be considered a step toward sainthood, I think.

But I thought you might be encouraged by seeing a glimpse of the personal discouragement I faced while trying to write the book you're holding. I seriously almost quit. I already told you about my episode on the flight back from Australia, but there were three other times too. The discouragement got so heavy I didn't think I could bear it.

The first crisis was determining what the book would be about—again.

I had already made the outline for a completely different book on a different topic. As I began to share about that book with different people, I realized that the subject was good but not gripping. It wasn't dealing with an issue that seemed immediately helpful to people. I think I'm trying to say that people found it boring.

So I trashed the concept, then the chatter took over, and I got stuck. I became convinced that I wasn't much of an author and that, although I had written two other books, I didn't have a third one in me.

But I have friends who pushed me to keep going. I also have publishers and contractual obligations. Furthermore, I knew there was a message I needed to get out. I just couldn't find the hook. Until one day when I was standing on the beach with a friend, watching the waves crash on the shore, cycling through every awful book title I've ever considered.

And it hit.

"Crash the Chatterbox," I said.

"Crash the who now?" my friend responded.

"Crash the *Chatterbox*," I repeated. "I think that's the title. Do you like it?"

"I love it," he responded.

And that was solved.

But the only thing harder than figuring out what to write about is writing it. After outlining the book over the course of a couple of days, I wrote nothing for months. In the busyness of pastoring a church, preparing sermons, and serving as CEO of the Furtick family, I totally lost sight of the book.

By the time I locked myself in a lodge in Montana to begin hammering it out, I literally couldn't produce a paragraph. For two days. I went on strikes against showers and stayed up until 5:00 a.m. so I could have extra time to stare at my blank screen. But no inspiration came.

Until the very last day of the trip, when all the discarded sentences I had forced out began to arrange themselves into a decent, readable first draft of a first chapter.

Well, I had a start. I headed home and worked on the book in brief spells for the next several months. And by the time the book was halfway done, I had a plan to finish it on time. I rented a house at the lake where I could take my family for a month and slay this sucker. Away from the daily responsibilities of the church and the weekly pressure of sermon prep, I knew I could knock it out.

We arrived at the lake, I set up my writing porch, wrote my time line on index cards and tacked it to a corkboard, and went to bed, planning to start a serial writing spree the next morning.

That night, around midnight, I got a call from my mom. She told me my father's medical condition had taken a sudden turn. He had only hours to live.

L-Train's Last Stop

Dad had been suffering from a fatal disease called ALS for more than eighteen months, so the call was not a surprise. But it came much sooner than we expected.

I returned home to be with my parents, and for the next three days I had the privilege of being by my dad's side as he spent his final hours in this world. The end of his life marked the conclusion of a very painful yet beautifully redemptive story that cannot possibly be contained in the space of this chapter. But I will try to share a few scenes.

My dad loved Southern Gospel music, so his memorial was a celebratory send-off that would rival any Gaither Homecoming. His name was Larry, but we all called him L-Train. So I preached a eulogy titled "This Train" based on the passage in 2 Corinthians we read earlier in this chapter. He had asked me before he died to make sure his story was told in a way that would give God the glory, so I thought that passage was perfect to show how, even though the L-Train came off the tracks sometimes, he kept rolling.

I wanted everyone to see how my dad treasured Christ in his life more than anything else but also how he carried the cargo of his faith in "jars of clay." I knew he wanted the story of his life "to show that this all-surpassing power is from God and not from us."

So I testified about how, against all odds, the L-Train finished his life as a man who deeply loved Christ and how he had a family who loved him by his side as he pulled into the station to receive his eternal reward.

I did my best to share truthfully about some of the dangers, toils, and snares that the L-Train had come through—sometimes as a result of his own disobedience, sometimes because of factors outside his control. But most of all, I wanted to show how, by God's grace, no matter how rough the ride was, *the train kept rolling.* God's grace never ran out on my dad.

I started by telling how, on his seventh birthday, L-Train found his father dead—a suicide.

And how as a boy he spent two years in a reform school, where he would be thrown into solitary for days at a time.

I shared how he dropped out of school in the eighth grade and became a juvenile delinquent, addicted to drugs and alcohol. This was the beginning of an addiction that he would battle for the rest of his life.

Still, the train kept rolling.

I talked about how he didn't know what to do when he became a teenage dad, especially since he had no father to show him how it was done. And I shared how, when he was fired by the company he thought he'd be with for the rest of his life, he didn't know how he was going to feed his family.

But he opened up a little barbershop in Moncks Corner, and somehow the train kept rolling. His family was always well provided for.

I explained how in his forties and fifties he had two tumors removed from his liver, followed by a liver transplant, and then two unsuccessful rounds of interferon treatment for hepatitis C. I talked about how he suffered from diabetic neuropathy so severe that his feet and back constantly burned.

But by God's grace, the train kept rolling.

And then I shared how, in the last three years of his life, after he'd gone to eight different specialists trying to find out why he couldn't stop twitching, his greatest fear was confirmed when he was diagnosed with ALS—a progressive neurodegenerative disease that kills most patients in two to three years.

The hardest part of the eulogy was finding an appropriate way to explain how, in the first year of his diagnosis, his anxiety and fear and anger drove him to a point of complete insanity. My dad became volatile—threatening his wife and several others, including me.

Ultimately, he ended up living alone for a period of several months, separated from his family in some of the darkest days our family has ever experienced.

But even when it looked as if he'd lost everything, he never lost his love for Jesus or his family. We never heard him curse God one time, although we heard him curse all of us quite a few times.

Yet even when he was unable to show it with his actions, we all knew his real desire; he wanted nothing more than for his family to be beside him in the final season of his life.

And we were. Because God is faithful and because my dad's wife of more than thirty years meant her wedding vows, my dad finally made it back to Charlotte, where he was restored to his family and cared for by my mom in his last months on earth.

These would be his most excruciating months. He would never dress or feed himself again. The man who had weighed close to three hundred pounds most of my life would shrink to less than half that. At every opportunity I liked to remind him that I could finally take him in a fight.

The man who had cut hair for more than twenty years and had provided a large percentage of the population of Moncks Corner with bowl cuts, buzz cuts, crew cuts, faux hawks, flattops, high and tights, rat tails, and mullets couldn't shave his own face or even comb his own hair. We affectionately referred to the season when he stopped shaving as his Charles Manson days.

At first he couldn't walk from one room to the next. Eventually he couldn't leave the bed, scratch his own itches, turn over, or reach up to tap the screen of the iPad that had been his lifeline to the world as the disease had progressed. He couldn't pass a bowel movement without help. And in the last three days of his life, as he struggled to breathe, he couldn't even speak to tell us what hurt.

As he drifted in and out of semiconsciousness, I decided to put his Martin guitar to use and sing medleys of his favorite hymns and gospel songs. The longer he hung in there, the more obscure the songs got. It was fun trying to remember as many songs about heaven as I could. When I ran out of songs about heaven, I mixed in some CCR. My mom and Holly helped me with the harmonies. My brother isn't much of a singer, but he was there.

And I told those who were gathered at the memorial about how, as I lay beside him in his bed, reading him a sermon by Charles Spurgeon called "The Peculiar Sleep of the Beloved," watching as he finally took his last breath, my sadness about his suffering gave way to rejoicing.

Because death is not the end of the line for a believer.

And even though my dad is gone, *the train is still rolling...*

When I got to this point in my eulogy, the crowd was on their feet. And together as a church family, we celebrated the life of a man who was "hard pressed on every side, but not crushed; perplexed, but not in despair; persecuted, but not abandoned; struck down, but not destroyed."[3]

At the conclusion of the service, we gave away $61,000 in his honor (he would have turned sixty-one in just a couple of weeks) to the outreach organizations that were especially meaningful to him. And we gave a train-shaped wooden whistle to each of the thousand people who had come to celebrate his life. Everybody blew them in unison as the band played "I Saw the Light."

It was one of the most moving events I've ever been a part of. And when it was over, I felt a tremendous sense of peace and relief, knowing my father had finally made it to heaven and will never hurt again. I also sensed the grace of God in the way the story ended, knowing that, as hard as it was, the result could have been so much worse.

I had so much to be thankful for.

All Aboard

When I made the trip back to the lake house, though, and walked onto my makeshift writing porch and saw the writing schedule on the corkboard, I realized how far behind I was. And discouragement hit.

Like a freight train.

Even after I had taken a few days off, when I opened my MacBook, I couldn't get any words flowing. I started making a plan to beg the publisher to push the release date a few months. Then I again began to entertain the option of scrapping the idea of the book altogether. A chorus of chatter was filling my mind with reasons to quit. But another voice inside me said, in a whisper, *Keep rolling.*

It may sound dumb to you, like the locomotive version of Dory's advice to Marlin. But that's what I needed to hear, and that's what I needed to do.

That simple impression overpowered the chatterbox long enough for me to write new note cards, breaking all the writing I had left to do into smaller assignments.

At first I wrote some stuff that was unbearably bad, then some stuff that was a little better, and in the weeks that followed, I kept rewriting until this book was the best I had to offer.

And you're holding it in your hands. No, it's not Dickens. But it's done. For this project I crashed the chatterbox. I kept rolling. I fulfilled God's purpose to deliver this message in this season of my life. I did it through confusion, self-doubt, and even the death of my dad. By God's grace I kept rolling.

Not that the discouragement I had to push through could be considered a dark night of the soul. But it was real to me, and it almost succeeded in preventing me from going forward. In my clash with discouragement, though, I learned something I'll carry with me the rest of my life.

God's grace doesn't clear the tracks of discouragement and setbacks.

It gives me the power to override the reasons I should stop.

And keep rolling.

The day I started writing again, I took my boys out to ride a Jet Ski. I'd been grinding all day and needed a break to clear my head.

We were exploring the different coves on the lake and naming them. I was trying to have a good time, but my mind was back on the writing porch. I was still having a hard time believing I actually had what it took to get the job done—to overpower my own chatter—and write a book worth reading.

Eventually we came upon a cove that was tucked behind a train trestle.

"This one's AWESOME!" Elijah shouted.

"Yeah, let's name it L-Train Cove," Graham replied.

Moments after he said this, we heard a rumbling sound, followed by a small black train passing by fewer than fifty yards in front of us.

I got the message.

I hope you're getting it too.

If you are a believer who hopes to accomplish the will of God for your life—and go to the next level spiritually—you have to defy the inertia of internal discouragement to get there. Whether you're a missionary in Calcutta, an apostle to the Gentiles, a barber in Moncks Corner, or that barber's son trying to write a book about how to hear God's voice above all others—you can't let the chatter stop you.

You have to keep rolling. And God says you can.

Now let's talk about how.

MY JOY IS NOT DETERMINED
BY WHAT HAPPENS TO ME,
BUT WHAT CHRIST IS DOING
IN ME AND THROUGH ME.

#CRASHTHECHATTERBOX

12

The Expectation Gap

You're born. You suffer. You die. Fortunately, there's a loophole.

—Billy Graham

So you don't intend to establish orphanages or write two-thirds of the New Testament. That doesn't mean you don't need a battle plan against discouragement. Chatter attacks everybody. It affects those who have public, visible roles in the kingdom of God, as we've seen. But it also affects those who have less prominent yet equally significant roles in the eyes of the Lord.

Every Christian has a calling. And the chatterbox is assigned to interrupt that calling. The ability to overcome discouragement is driven by our intentional decision to reassure ourselves: *God says I can.* This is especially crucial at the times when the chatter is most convincingly overwhelming us with reasons why we can't.

Holly used to teach fifth grade, and I used to take her lunch sometimes. One day I walked into her classroom, and I felt like I was in a scene straight out of *Sister Act 2.* The kids were singing a gospel song I'd never heard, called "Yes, I Can." It was quite inspirational to see them all singing such a positive message, until Holly explained to me that the principal had mandated they sing it in preparation for end-of-grade testing. After this discovery the "Yes, I can" chorus was less convincing.

Listen, I'm aware it may feel a little predictable at this point in the book for me to pump you up with a confession as simple as *God says I can.* But even if it seems forced at first, it's vital that you train your heart to confess this with conviction.

Your destiny depends on it.

####

When the internal dialogue of discouragement starts in your heart, remember—the Enemy's goal goes way beyond putting you in a bad mood temporarily. He's trying to talk you out of trusting God's plan for your life at a foundational level. And he's not just trying to derail *you*. He aims to limit the impact God wants to make through you and beyond you.

Discouragement can gradually undermine your passion for raising your children, for example. It can leave you feeling and behaving more like a warden than a shepherd. And, yes, you'll miss opportunities to enjoy your children, and you'll regret this. But that's only one dimension of what you'll miss.

You'll also miss the opportunity to partner with God in preparing them for their destiny. Who knows what great works your children are capable of for God's glory? As a parent, you are God's agent—appointed to help steward their calling.

But when you allow discouragement to bring you down, the gravitational pull seizes them too. The Enemy attacks *them* by telling *you*:

Nothing you say to them ever sticks anyway. It's not working, so what's the point?

They don't appreciate you and probably never will. It's not working, so what's the point?

It doesn't matter whether you take them to church. It's not working, so what's the point?

Other parents don't try nearly as hard and don't struggle nearly as much. It's not working, so what's the point?

I'm using one example—parenting—to illustrate a universal feature of discouragement. Discouragement shows up in multiple ways. It can set in because of what others say or what they don't say, what they do or don't do. It can hit as hard when we're winning as when we're losing—remember Elijah in the cave? Sometimes it comes like a flood; sometimes it drips incessantly.

But regardless of how or when it arrives, discouragement always displaces hope and leaves you feeling something like this: *It's not working, so what's the point?*

Haven't you felt this way at work? at school? on the elliptical? in church? while reading this book? in a conversation with someone you love?

Defeating discouragement is largely about understanding the stakes. It's largely about understanding the implications of your obedience—beyond you.

But rejecting the chatter of discouragement and persisting instead in the purposes of God also requires choosing to believe what He has said, whether you can hear it right now or not.

The Most Encouraging Message You've Never Heard

Someone asked me recently, "What's the greatest source of discouragement you've faced in ministry so far?"

My first answer was "people," but I was only kidding. I was kind of kidding. Then I gave him a more serious answer: "The greatest source of discouragement for me is going through pain when I can't see the purpose." What I meant was, I don't get very discouraged when I'm exhausted or hurting—as long as I can see that what I'm doing is *working.*

I don't mind sacrifice as long as it produces a greater gain. I don't grow weary in welldoing, as long as the work I'm doing produces tangible results. It's not pouring myself out for a worthy purpose that depletes me. What's draining is giving my all and seeming to get nothing in return.

I have a sermon I love to preach about John the Baptist. I call it "The Most Encouraging Message You've Never Heard." I love to preach it because it's uplifting and simple. These are my three points:

1. You're doing better than you think you are.
2. It's less about you than you think it is.
3. You matter more than you think you do.

As I preach these points, I ask the people in the audience to participate by preaching them back to one another. And then I tell them to take these points home and regularly preach them to *themselves.* Because discouragement will arrive at the doorstep of your mind as certainly as a Cialis commercial will air during the Masters. Okay, a wings commercial during *Sunday Night Football*— is that more appropriate?

But the presence of extreme discouragement isn't necessarily an indication that you're not doing the will of God. In fact, the secret struggles of John the Baptist, just like those of Mother Teresa and the apostle Paul, prove the opposite.

Inner conflict is often a *confirmation* of your calling. The Enemy only fights those who pose a threat.

If you're not sick of my preacher lines, permit me one more: If you haven't had a head-on collision with the devil lately, it may be because you're running in the same direction.

Say "amen," somebody.

But discouragement need not be a dead end. Properly navigated, it can become a doorway to discovering the comfort and courage of Christ in untold measures.

In Matthew's gospel we see John the Baptist's discouragement surfacing in the form of a question:

> After Jesus had finished instructing his twelve disciples, he went on
> from there to teach and preach in the towns of Galilee.
>
> When John, who was in prison, heard about the deeds of the
> Messiah, he sent his disciples to ask him, "Are you the one who is
> to come, or should we expect someone else?" (Matthew 11:1–3)

Evidently, John's confidence in Christ is progressing, full speed, in the wrong direction. Understandably so. While Jesus is busy dazzling crowds on His regional speaking/healing/deliverance/miracle tour, John is rotting on death row. As he serves an unjust prison sentence because of his stand for righteousness, John is missing out on fulfilling the mission he was a part of inaugurating.

After all, it was John who had announced,

> After me comes one who is more powerful than I, whose sandals I am
> not worthy to carry. He will baptize you with the Holy Spirit and fire.
> (Matthew 3:11)

So when John sends a few of his staff members to ask Jesus, as directly as possible, "Are you the one?" it's surprising.

There's nothing strange or unique about the question—*everyone* is wondering at some level about the true identity of the prophet from Galilee. He's a profound teacher, to be sure, and that thing with the fish and loaves was a *heck of a deal*, but is He the *One*? the Messiah? the Savior of the world?

Or should we expect another?

It's a reasonable question to investigate. But it seems bizarre to hear the very one who had announced the reign of Christ now questioning the ministry he had boldly announced.

To be clear, nothing in the text suggests that John was denying Christ or compromising his convictions. And this is important to point out, because the chatterbox will try to use your questions about the way God is working in your life to accuse you of weak faith. We've already seen how counterproductive that kind of condemnation, powered by accusation, is to our relationship with God.

I've heard people claim that John's question was a result of spiritual immaturity on his part. But that assumption doesn't hold up. As we're about to see, Jesus has some pretty complimentary things to say about John.

John's discouragement isn't due to a lack of belief. It is the result of an unmet expectation.

See, when John commended Jesus to the crowds, he did so with a certain expectation. He expected that Christ would conduct a ministry of judgment. He explained how Jesus had His "winnowing fork...in his hand" and how he would "clear his threshing floor, gathering his wheat into the barn." He assured the people that Jesus would be "burning up the chaff with unquenchable fire."[1] His expectation was that the vindication of God's people and the cause of righteousness would be swift and severe.

Now, as John languishes in Herod's prison, disappointment is setting in. John has done his part—scorching the Pharisees, even rebuking Herod himself. But from what he's hearing, Jesus isn't doing any scorching. When John introduced "the Lamb of God, who takes away the sin of the world,"[2] he had no doubts. But Jesus was not taking away the sin of the world in the way John had hoped he would. How could He deliver His people when, so far, He appeared to be the type who wouldn't bust a grape in a fruit fight?

In other words, John had spent himself to do the work of the Lord. But from his vantage point, *it wasn't working*. Now he's wondering, *What's the point?*

Let me offer a working definition of *disappointment*: disappointment is the gap between what I expect and what I experience. And the chatterbox looks for ways to exploit your disappointment by filling that gap with doubts about the goodness of God.

God wouldn't let you go through this if He loved you.

This wouldn't be happening if you had more faith.

If it were possible for things to change, they'd have changed by now.

Disappointed expectations, when full-grown, give birth to chronic discouragement. If you allow this discouragement to run rampant in your life, you'll lose your hope.

God in the Gap

So how do you manage the gap between the chatterbox's claim that you can't and God's insistence that you can?

Some choose to pretend it doesn't exist. When faced with a disappointment, they deny its effects and pretend everything is fine. But nobody is immune to discouragement. And if all you do is hide the symptoms, your hope still dies. It just dies silently.

Ignoring the gap won't produce transformation. It will only postpone the reality of frustration, allowing it to pick up momentum. Then when the frustration finally hits—and it will—it will be devastating because it wasn't dealt with in a realistic yet faith-filled way.

Others, instead of ignoring the gap, give up in the gap. Sick of being let down, they simply lower their expectations to the level of their experience. And then they start to live by mantras like "Well, I'll hope for the best, but I expect the worst."

Something goes wrong, and their auto reply is "Story of my life."

Giving in to discouragement pacifies your disappointment—at first. Then you realize the pacifier is poisonous, because as believers, when we lower our expectation to the level of our experience, we factor God out of the equation. Instead of looking for His favor in every situation, we begin to anticipate the outcomes we dread. And since much of our experience is regulated by the level of our expectation, we begin to get what we were expecting. And we're not surprised.

It's the chicken and the egg. Which came first? The lowered expectation? Or the lackluster result? (Does it matter? Either way we're hopeless.)

Ignore the gap. Give up in the gap. I've done both. And both backfire every time.

I want to train myself to do what John the Baptist did: I want to learn, more and more, to allow God to fill the gap.

John took his disappointed expectation to the only One with the authority to appropriately address it. That's a great example for us to follow. Few of us will suffer the kind of persecution John did. But that doesn't make our frustrations any less acute. It doesn't make our real-time, real-life disappointments any less pertinent.

My father-in-law has a great line he used to tell Holly all the time. He wanted to make sure she set her standards high and held out for the right man. Obviously, this was a successful campaign. Anyway, he'd tell her, "Holly, there's only one thing worse than being single and lonely. And that's being married and lonely."

He was trying to help her see that, in marriage, expectation and experience can be as far apart as the health benefits of kale chips and Doritos. He wanted her to understand that it's not just unmarried people who feel frustrated.

When you expect to get married by a certain age, and it doesn't happen, it can be devastating to your expectations. Often this is because the expectation we place on marriage is a faulty one. The wedding day is, after all, supposed to inaugurate an era of contentment, harmony, a shared Netflix account, and total-life happiness. *You had me at hello, and now you complete me.*

But it's not quite like that. When two incomplete people come together, expecting the other to make them whole, the result is not wholeness. Instead the marriage creates a shared brokenness, which results in resentment and misery.

Holly's dad was trying to raise a daughter who not only would have the right expectations but also would place her expectations on the right person—Jesus. In fact, both of Holly's parents worked very hard to teach her what it meant to be complete in Christ. That's one of the things I found most attractive about her when we were dating. She was the kind of girl who let God fill her gaps.

Allowing God to fill your gaps means refusing to pretend the gaps don't exist. But it also means refusing to attempt to fill the gaps in ways—or with people—that can't get the job done.

Only God is big enough to fill the gap.

####

A friend recently turned me on to a little book featuring the correspondence between Rainer Maria Rilke, a famous Austrian poet, and a younger aspiring poet Rilke was seeking to encourage. The book is entitled, appropriately, *Letters to a Young Poet.*

The young poet was struggling through military school—the same school

Rilke had attended—and was locked in cycles of discouragement. Rilke admonished him in one passage that was especially moving to me:

> You are so young, all beginning is so far in front of you, and I should like
> to beg you earnestly to have patience with all unsolved problems in your
> heart and to try to love the questions themselves like locked rooms, or
> books that are written in a foreign tongue. Do not search now for the
> answers, which cannot be given you, because you could not live them.
> That is the point, to live everything. Now you must live your problems.
> And perhaps gradually, without noticing it, you will live your way into
> the answer some distant day.[3]

Living your problems and loving them like locked rooms is much different from denying them or capitulating to them. It is believing that God is *with* you in the imperfect, even disappointing circumstances of your life.

It is saying to Him with faith in your heart, *You will, and therefore I can.*

Approval Rating

John the Baptist may have been discouraged. But he wasn't derailed by his discouragement. He stuffed his pain in a box with packing peanuts and FedExed the whole package to Jesus.

Jesus sent the messengers back to John with this reply:

> The blind receive sight, the lame walk, those who have leprosy are
> cleansed, the deaf hear, the dead are raised, and the good news is
> proclaimed to the poor. Blessed is anyone who does not stumble on
> account of me. (Matthew 11:5–6)

But Jesus didn't stop there. "As John's disciples were leaving, Jesus began to speak to the crowd about John." Here is what He said:

> What did you go out into the wilderness to see? A reed swayed by the
> wind? If not, what did you go out to see? A man dressed in fine clothes?

No, those who wear fine clothes are in kings' palaces. Then what did you go out to see? A prophet? Yes, I tell you, and more than a prophet. This is the one about whom it is written:

> "I will send my messenger ahead of you,
>   who will prepare your way before you."

Truly I tell you, among those born of women there has not risen anyone greater than John the Baptist; yet whoever is least in the kingdom of heaven is greater than he. (verses 7–11)

Talk about a celebrity endorsement. What a reassuring affirmation! Hearing those words spoken about him must have fortified John in unimaginable ways. *The greatest born of a woman! More than a prophet!*

John had sent Jesus a question: "Are you the one?" Instead of answering that question directly, Jesus confirms John's calling to the whole crowd. Speaking of John, Jesus says, "This is the one about whom it is written." And He goes on to offer proof after glowing proof about the validity and effectiveness of John's ministry.

While John is wondering whether Jesus is the One, confused by circumstances that seem to point to the contrary, Jesus wants to make sure everyone in attendance that day knows that *John* is still the one. John was, and is, the chosen messenger to prepare the way of the Lord. Not only does Jesus not criticize John for asking the question; He turns the question inside out, using it as an opportunity to esteem John publicly.

Undoubtedly, it bolstered John's belief in the mission to hear that such things were being said about him.

Except that John never heard any of it.

Behind Your Back

The first time I realized this, it blew my mind. In the text we read earlier, Jesus's response to John is divided into two sections. And those two sections are divided by a few inconspicuous but all-important words in verse 7:

As John's disciples were leaving, Jesus began to speak to the crowd about John.

In verses 4–6, Jesus instructs John's messengers to give John the status report he asked for. But notice, there's nothing in the report about how great John is. The report is all about what Jesus is doing. And the instruction is for John to endure.

Then after John's disciples are out of earshot, Jesus starts bragging about John, heaping accolade upon accolade on the ministry of this faithful man.

Which leads me to ask a question. Why did Jesus wait until John's messengers were gone to start highlighting John's significance in the kingdom? Wouldn't this be the kind of stuff you'd want somebody to hear if you were trying to motivate him to endure?

Instead, Jesus in essence talks about John behind his back. Apparently, Jesus doesn't want John to hear the next part. If so, He'd say it before the disciples split.

Make sure John knows he's a total rock star.

But apparently Jesus doesn't want John's confidence to rest in John. Jesus structures the message in such a way that John's confidence can only rest in Jesus.

"Jesus began to speak *to* the crowd *about* John…"

The only motivation to endure that John is given is based on the work Christ is doing, not the work John has done, as remarkable as it is.

Is it possible that when we're not getting the affirmation or confirmation we desire, it's because God doesn't want our faith to rest in affirmation we can feel? In these times could it be that He's at work on a deeper level, teaching us to rely on His character rather than our performance?

"Go back and report to John what you hear and see: The blind receive sight, the lame walk, those who have leprosy are cleansed."

I wonder what God has been saying behind your back lately. Unlike John, we're not dependent on a courier to relay the message to us. The Holy Spirit, who is inside you, lives to testify with your spirit, affirming you in this moment:

You're doing better than you think you are.

It's less about you than you think it is.

You matter more than you think you do. More than you could ever know.

It's working. It's not in vain.

Don't stop.

The chatter of discouragement is so noticeable and constant. Sometimes, by contrast, the affirmation of God can seem so hidden and sporadic.

Especially in the gap.

Maybe the gap between what you expected in this season of your life and what you're experiencing is a chasm that seems too wide to cross. Even with God's help.

It's okay to feel that way. It's permissible, even noble, to strain to believe what God has said when you're standing in the gap, wondering what in the world He's doing and when He will come through for you.

But it's no reason for you to fall away.

Surely the gap is no wider for you than it was for John.

As it turns out, from a human standpoint there is to be no happy ending in John's story. The gap is never reconciled, at least not in this life and not in the way I would have expected.

After hearing about John's bout with discouragement, wouldn't you expect Jesus to take action—break Cousin John out of prison? If Andy Dufresne can do it…

Instead, Scripture records that Herod "had John beheaded in the prison. His head was brought in on a platter and given to the girl, who carried it to her mother. John's disciples came and took his body and buried it. Then they went and told Jesus."[4]

Could this even remotely resemble the ending John expected? When Jesus stepped onto the scene, and John urged his followers to follow Jesus the Christ instead, did he know that his gesture of worship and selflessness would be remunerated with a criminal's execution?

When he declared in John 3:30, "He [Jesus] must become greater; I must become less," could he possibly have imagined that becoming less would mean going *this* low and losing his very *life*? No, Jesus didn't kill John, but He allowed him to be killed. Either way, John's dead. It is highly unlikely that John foresaw any of these events playing out the way they did.

Even so, he didn't let what he expected keep him from what Jesus wanted him to experience. He stayed faithful in life and even unto death. And as a result, he accomplished the purpose of God in a way no one else ever would. Just as John had the privilege of preparing the way for Jesus in life, so he would prepare the way for Jesus in death.

It wouldn't be long before Jesus, suffering a death much more savage and humiliating than John experienced, would give John this affirmation: "Well done, good and faithful servant."

Not through a messenger, but face to face.

Not in this life, but in the life that will never end.

Not in the way John would have expected, but in a way that would exceed anything John could have ever asked or imagined.

If God always met our expectations, He'd never be able to exceed them. Sometimes God takes us to another level by building higher. Sometimes He does it by digging deeper. But at all times He is working for the good of those who love Him and are called according to His purpose.

The Joy of Holland

Holly's mom, Deborah, shared with me several years ago an experience she had with Joy, her youngest daughter. Joy is a beautiful young lady who was born with special needs.

In my opinion, parenting presents the highest degree of relational difficulty. But being the parent of a child with special needs must complicate the decision-making process of parenting exponentially. *How do I care for this child, considering—but not overcompensating for—her needs? How do I give her freedom but also protection? How do I normalize her life, knowing that life for her will never be normal?*

Holly's parents continue to deal with these questions daily, even now that Joy is thirty years old.

But there have been certain transitional points in the journey of raising Joy where the discouragement has been deafening for Deborah. One of those points came when Joy was about to turn fifteen. Parents of other fifteen-year-olds were preparing their daughters for their driving tests, teaching them to parallel park. And the discouragement started detonating in Deborah's heart: *Your daughter will probably never drive a vehicle.* And she wouldn't.

Other girls were starting to go out on dates. Deborah was trying to determine how best to explain to Joy why she might not be asked out on dates while showing her that she was valuable and beautiful.

Deborah had pushed through the chatter concerning various stages of Joy's development. But with each growth spurt and developmental delay came more discouragement.

One day when the confusion seemed unbearable, Deborah came across an essay titled "Welcome to Holland".by Emily Perl Kingsley. It didn't solve all the tensions of disappointment for Deborah. And it won't for you. But it's a brilliant lens to look through for any disappointment you're facing.

Kingsley writes,

I am often asked to describe the experience of raising a child with a disability—to try to help people who have not shared that unique experience to understand it, to imagine how it would feel. It's like this…

When you're going to have a baby, it's like planning a fabulous vacation trip—to Italy. You buy a bunch of guide books and make your wonderful plans. The Coliseum. The Michelangelo David. The gondolas in Venice. You may learn some handy phrases in Italian. It's all very exciting.

After months of eager anticipation, the day finally arrives. You pack your bags and off you go. Several hours later, the plane lands. The flight attendant comes in and says, "Welcome to Holland."

"Holland?!?" you say. "What do you mean Holland?? I signed up for Italy! I'm supposed to be in Italy. All my life I've dreamed of going to Italy."

But there's been a change in the flight plan. They've landed in Holland and there you must stay.

The important thing is that they haven't taken you to a horrible, disgusting, filthy place, full of pestilence, famine and disease. It's just a different place.

So you must go out and buy new guide books. And you must learn a whole new language. And you will meet a whole new group of people you would never have met.

It's just a *different* place. It's slower-paced than Italy, less flashy than Italy. But after you've been there for a while and you catch your breath, you look around…and you begin to notice that Holland has windmills…and Holland has tulips. Holland even has Rembrandts.

But everyone you know is busy coming and going from Italy…and they're all bragging about what a wonderful time they had there. And for the rest of your life, you will say "Yes, that's where I was supposed to go. That's what I had planned."

And the pain of that will never, ever, ever, ever go away…because the loss of that dream is a very very significant loss.

But…if you spend your life mourning the fact that you didn't get to Italy, you may never be free to enjoy the very special, the very lovely things…about Holland.[5]

Don't let what you expected keep you from what God wants you to experience. God has plans for you that you know nothing about right now. That means He may take you down paths that seem to lead to nowhere.

Believing God means assuming that He is always working, even when our faith and prayers and love don't seem to be working at all. Realizing this opens our hearts to accept what God has allowed in each season of our lives without being overtaken by discouragement. The more we can rest in this confidence, the wider our spiritual eyes will open to the blessings the Father has already given us.

And this kind of gratitude—the kind that does not shrink back but fights back in the face of discouragement—is kryptonite to the chatterbox.

DON'T LET WHAT YOU EXPECTED
KEEP YOU FROM WHAT GOD WANTS
YOU TO EXPERIENCE.

#CRASHTHECHATTERBOX

13

The Parable of the Passport

Cultivate thankfulness. Let the Word of Christ—the Message—have
the run of the house.

—THE APOSTLE PAUL, COLOSSIANS 3:16, MSG

Maybe it's because I'm from the South, or maybe it's because I'm unusually uptight, but I'm a stickler for manners. I freely confess that when I hear someone under the age of eighteen respond to an adult without the courtesy of a *ma'am* or a *sir,* my face tenses, my teeth grind, and I almost reflexively reach to turn them over my knee.

I make no claim that my kids are poster children for good manners, but Holly and I do enforce certain protocols. Perhaps this obsession subconsciously started when my grandmother shoved an entire bar of soap in my mouth after hearing me speak dishonorably toward my mom one day at lunch. I presume Alzheimer's erased this incident from her memory, but I'll remember it until the day I die.

Whatever the reason, I have a strong conviction in parenting to teach my kids that mistakes are inevitable but disrespect is inexcusable. And ingratitude is more than a misdemeanor.

The words *sir* and *ma'am* are not optional around the Furtick house, and neither are *please* and *thank you.* If you want to eat, or breathe, and avoid a generally unpleasant life, you will learn to use those words fluently. You must speak the language of respect and appreciation in our home, or it will not go well with you in your days on the earth. It may sound old school, but I feel these values are more important than ever, considering that a culture of dishonor and ingratitude seems to be on the rise.

Just as many children never receive or embrace basic principles about honor and thankfulness, many of God's children never understand that approaching God involves a certain protocol as well. It is a protocol that is countercultural and kind of counterintuitive. It is a language and posture that is grounded in respect and appreciation. It contradicts the constant chatter of discouragement, and it attunes our hearts to God's voice in every circumstance.

I'm not suggesting God wants us to fuss endlessly over the exact wording of our prayers in order to satisfy a must-be-this-tall-to-ride requirement before we pray. Jesus condemned the sort of rigid formality that was in vogue in His day, instructing His disciples to instead address God as Father. Through Christ, we can come to God the Father as we are, knowing He will receive us as His children.

But the same God we know as Father and Friend is also the King of the universe. And this King has given us specific instructions for how to come into His presence—not because His ego needs to be appeased, but because our perspective needs to be corrected. The psalmist instructs us to

> Enter his gates with thanksgiving
>   and his courts with praise;
>   give thanks to him and praise his name.
> For the LORD is good and his love endures forever;
>   his faithfulness continues through all generations.
>   (Psalm 100:4–5)

Often these verses are applied to the contexts of corporate worship gatherings or personal prayer techniques. This book is not primarily focused on either of those subjects, obviously. But still, the psalmist presents an important truth for us. When we enter the gates of God's presence with thanksgiving, we survey the wonderful things He's already done. This sense of gratitude combats our discouragement by reestablishing our confidence:

If God did it before, I'll do it again.
If God says I can, I can.

Nothing will bring us into a consciousness of God's presence more quickly and deeply than praising Him and giving thanks to Him. And nothing will disrupt our awareness of His presence like focusing on our own discontent.

Stuck like Buck

One of my most valuable sidekicks in ministry is a guy named Buck. He's part bouncer, part prayer warrior, part travel wizard, part physical trainer, part ministry assistant. He's also one of my best friends. I've known him since college. We've done a lot of cool stuff together. Once we were chased out of a Chinese discotheque together. He's one of the most reliable travel team members a pastor could have.

Except one time.

A while back, on the Monday after Easter, we were scheduled to leave from my house to go on a week-long ministry trip. We were headed to Sydney, Australia. (This was the same trip where I gave my boys a sneak preview of the future, à la Marty McFly.)

The rest of the team was busy loading stuff into the vehicles when Buck asked if he could talk with me privately. The look on his face let me know he wasn't pulling me aside to thank me for the opportunity or to quote a few lines from *Crocodile Dundee* or to usher in the Spirit of Oz as we embarked upon our journey.

"Pastor, I can't find my passport," he said.

I nodded slowly so as not to appear frustrated. He was already flustered and embarrassed enough.

"Well, what are you going to do?" I asked.

His response was an instant classic. "I guess I'll just fly from Charlotte to L.A. with you guys and see what happens when we get there."

Buck and I both knew what would happen when he got to customs with no passport and attempted to board a plane bound for the other side of the world.

And that's exactly what did happen.

The rest of the team continued on to Sydney. Buck headed off, alone, in the middle of the night, to rent a car. After a few hours of sleep in a pay-by-the-hour hotel (okay, I made up that part for effect), Buck arrived at the customs office. After waiting almost all day there, Buck was the proud possessor of a special-issue passport.

He took the next flight to Australia and joined the team a day late, exhausted—and still furious with himself.

When he arrived, the conference I was preaching at was already in full swing. I happened to be speaking about gratitude in the first session he attended. And as I read Psalm 100:4—the part about entering His gates with thanksgiving—I thought about Buck's passport. On the spur of the moment, I decided to turn this little passport predicament into a preaching illustration.

"Buck, stand up," I said.

And in front of a few thousand Aussies, with Buck standing red-faced the whole time on the front row, I shared the parable of the passport.

"Praise is like a passport," I explained after telling the story in vivid detail and getting more laughs than Letterman—at Buck's expense.

"Buck flew all the way across the country and sincerely desired to go on to his destination...had a good reason to go on...had the resources to go on. But how many know that without a passport you're not getting past the gate?

Key〉 "And I came to let you know today that without praise, God says, you're not getting past the gate. '*Enter* his gates with thanksgiving and his courts with *praise*.'"

The people loved it. Buck was a good sport.

I thought, and still think, it was an excellent illustration of how gratitude gives us access to the places God wants to take us and enables the things He wants to do through us.

But it wasn't until dinner that night that the fullness of the parable of the passport was revealed to me.

As we were eating, reliving the afternoon session, I asked the crew, "How did you guys like that story about Buck?" I was rather proud of my impromptu illustration.

"It was classic, mate, and you didn't even tell the best part!" one of our ministry hosts volunteered.

"The best part?" I asked, clearly confused, but still smiling to give the appearance of omniscience.

Buck spoke up. "Well, I was waiting for a better time to tell you this, but there's a Part B to the story."

And Buck proceeded to tell me how, after he had gone through all the necessary steps to get a new passport issued, and while he was waiting in L.A. for the next available flight, he sat on a curb outside the passport office. In a half-praying, half-self-flagellating way, he was trying to figure out what lesson he needed to take away from this situation. Was God trying to teach him something?

How could you be so stupid, he was saying to himself as he banged his head on a leather notebook he carries with him everywhere. A notebook where he often keeps important documents. A notebook that contained, upon further inspection, his original passport tucked inside the back flap, a place Buck had not thought to look throughout this entire ordeal.

All the delay, discouragement, and dismay could have been avoided. The document he needed had never left his possession. It was on him the whole time.

I've now preached the parable of the passport all over the world. I always thank Buck, because the dumbest mistake he ever made turned out to be one of the greatest illustrations I've ever used.

But now when I preach it, I share the *full* meaning.

The truth is, many of us are stuck at the gate, *waiting for God to give us something that's already ours.* We're waiting for joy when God has given us the power to rejoice. We're waiting for encouragement to come to us when, in fact, the encouragement we need is locked in an opportunity God has given us to encourage someone else.

In the Furtick house my children are taught to say "please" when they want something and "thank you" when they get it. God puts things in a little different order. He teaches His children to say "thank You" for what we already have—as well as what we're expecting Him, by faith, to give—before we say "please" and ask Him for what we need next.

Obviously, God doesn't require us to rattle off a comprehensive list before granting us permission to pray. But before we ask God for *anything,* we should be thankful in *everything.*

So often we live as if our discouragement is a by-product of our difficulties. This leaves us feeling helpless in the throes of discouragement. And, to be sure, certain situations and setbacks are so challenging that they can knock the wind out of us. Not only does it become difficult to want to praise God, but it can seem impossible to do so.

But gratitude allows us to disconnect discouragement at the power source by choosing to call God good in spite of our situation.

Discontentment, on the other hand, will seize on hardship to paralyze our spiritual strength. It will even vandalize the great gifts God gives us by causing us to take them for granted.

Because, in actuality, gratitude is not based on how good my situation *is*.

It's based on how good my situation seems to me.

Come Out Like You Went In

We've talked about various ways of finding and replacing chatter. We've developed strategies to counteract forms of spiritual sabotage. But the one we're talking about now could be considered the Magna Carta Holy Grail.

Gratitude is a key that brings freedom, a weapon that brings victory, and a connection to limitless joy in all circumstances.

I'm not talking about the kind of gratitude that appreciates God only when things go our way. Even unbelievers tip their hats to deity when a little something comes their way—a bonus check, a snow day when they didn't study for exams, or a police officer who lets them slide this time.

I'm talking about a Christ-centered gratitude that crashes the chatterbox by replacing everything bad with something better—a present awareness of the goodness of God. This continuous gratitude scrambles the signal and disrupts the flow of discouragement. It changes your life, whether your situation changes immediately or not at all.

In Acts 16, Paul and Silas have every reason to be discouraged. They've just been stripped, humiliated, and flogged by Roman guards for preaching the gospel of Jesus. Now their feet are in stocks, their reputations are slandered, and their lives are in jeopardy. What do they do? Scripture records:

About midnight Paul and Silas were *praying and singing hymns* to God, and the other prisoners were listening to them. Suddenly there was such a violent earthquake that the foundations of the prison were shaken. At once all the prison doors flew open, and everyone's chains came loose. (verses 25–26, emphasis added)

How do you come out the prison of discouragement?
The same way you come into the presence of God: with praise.

Paul and Silas prove that the same gratitude the psalmist says brings you *into* God's presence has the power to bring you *out of* dismay, dejection, and disappointment.

It's not a magic trick. It doesn't mean if you'll say "Thank You, Jesus" thirty-three times a day for the next thirty days, you'll always be healed, rich, and in your ideal BMI range.

But gratitude does mean that, no matter how bad your situation is—whether mildly annoying or unspeakably agonizing—you have a secret passageway out of discouragement. Having a grateful attitude in adversity isn't living in denial; it's choosing to see your situation from a higher vantage point.

A spirit of discontent can make even the greatest blessing seem like a burden.

A spirit of gratitude can find a blessing within any burden.

Another Five Rounds

It is a rare thing to witness someone with this kind of gratitude, but it happens. And when you get a glimpse of it, you never forget it. It marks you, and if you'll let it, it transforms you.

I saw it when a couple on our church staff, Wade and Ferris, recently found out that their third daughter, Sydney, has cystic fibrosis. That's a devastating blow for any parent, but it seemed especially unfair to Wade and Ferris. Four years earlier Ferris had given birth three months prematurely to twin girls whose *combined* birthweight was less than five pounds. Wade and Ferris had been steadfast in their faith as one of the girls recovered from the most severe, grade-four brain bleed the doctors had ever seen. They had been resolute in believing that God would enable both girls to overcome the most dire diagnosis—that they might never talk, walk, or function normally.

I told the miraculous story of the Joye twins in *Sun Stand Still*.[1] It was a battle that included five initial surgeries, numerous infections, blood infusions, and sleepless nights in the hospital. But it has been an incredible victory. The twins turned five this month. Wade is currently reading them *The Lion, the Witch and the Wardrobe* at bedtime. They are fully functioning, princess-obsessed, constant reminders of the faithfulness of God.

But when I heard about Sydney's condition, it seemed incomprehensible that God would call on this couple, who had been so faithful in their last fight, to have to battle again so soon. Shouldn't the fight of your life be a once-in-a-lifetime occurrence? Why was this couple, who serve God with such passion, having to gear up for another five rounds in the Octagon?

I got the news as my flight from Miami to Charlotte was boarding, and I called Wade immediately. The plane was full and loud, and the flight attendant was instructing me to put away my phone, but I had to talk to Wade before we took off.

Wade answered the call on the first ring, prompt as always, and I could tell he was tired and disoriented. But he was also strangely and authentically grateful. He was saying things like "I'm just so thankful for the things God taught us in advance to prepare us for this," and "We just feel so blessed to be surrounded by people in our church who are lifting us up and covering us and standing with us."

He wasn't feeding me preprogrammed, disconnected lines in the style of South Carolina's 2007 Miss Teen USA contestant. He wasn't regurgitating these sentences in the way that many Christians have been trained to bluff their way through trials—"I hate my life, but praise the Lord!"

He was choosing to deal a deathblow to discouragement through the power of gratitude.

I know that with the symptoms and struggles Sydney will face, the Joyes' battle has just begun. Ahead of them lie challenges as parents and as a family that no one can measure from here—that we can hardly even imagine. But at the level of the spirit, I believe the victory is already theirs.

Can't Call It *reverse*

To paraphrase a quote I heard a long time ago, gratitude is thanking God in advance for what will only make sense in reverse. The chatter of discouragement is inevitable. The misery of discontent is not.

How do you overcome discouragement? Through gratitude. There is always something to thank God for once you've made the decision to be a grateful person.

I'm sure you've known people like Ferris and Wade who seem to find a blessing, enlarge a blessing, or create a blessing in almost any situation. And it's not just when the big stuff hits, like a worst-case-scenario medical diagnosis. They do it even in the humdrum hills and valleys of everyday life.

I saw this principle in motion one Sunday morning early in the history of our church. One of the founding members of Elevation, Larry Brey, came to see me backstage after the service was over. He brought with him his typical energy—loud and abounding, *put on a happy face, what a wonderful world.*

I was pouting and in no mood to be cheered up or be around anyone who was feeling happy. Attendance had been horrible that day due to heavy rain. That meant a break in momentum, a drop in the offering, and a valid excuse for the pastor to be in a bad mood. I honestly couldn't imagine any reason LB would have to be standing in my greenroom with that stupid smile on his face. What he said next was even more unforgivable.

"Now *that* was a great day!" he said, or rather shouted.

"Really?" I asked in disbelief. "And why is *that?*"

"Well, it's the first nasty storm we've had on a Sunday. And it gave our ushers a chance to shine. You should have seen them out there. They were like an army, getting people in out of the rain. It was *a-maz-ing* the way they honored our guests. Plus we finally got to use our custom Elevation umbrellas—they looked *sharp.*"

How can you stay down in the presence of a person like that? How can you pout around a guy who, instead of calling it a rainout, calls it an opportunity for our ushers to shine? I was simultaneously encouraged by his perspective and ashamed that he had to be the one to show me—his leader—the silver lining. I was also still a little annoyed by his Mr. Brightside demeanor, if you want to know the truth, probably because I was convicted by it.

I tend to be one of those people who takes great pride in calling it like I see it. I say things like,

"I'm not being grumpy or negative or pessimistic. I'm just keeping it real."

"I'm not complaining. I'm just calling it like I see it."

But people armed with a spirit of gratitude know that often it *is* what you *call* it.

So what if, instead of calling it like we see it, we began to call it like God *says* it?

If you call your schedule busy, hectic, and overwhelming, that's how it will feel. Your words will give weight to the very dread and discontent that the Enemy intends to use to discourage you. But if you call your schedule full and challenging yet fruitful, it will begin to take on those dimensions, first internally and then externally.

I have noticed that certain seasons of my life that had the potential to be the most stressful turned out to be the most joyful and productive because I disciplined myself to speak and think about them in terms of opportunity, not obligation.

I have also experienced the opposite far too many times.

If you call your job a dead end, that's exactly what it will become to you. Your work will seem stagnant; therefore, your passion will stagnate within the environment you have created with your attitude. But if you call your job a training ground and thank God for using it as a means of provision, God will see your faithfulness in little and in due time will make you faithful over much more.

This morning I caught myself yelling at my kids, "Come on, you don't have to be so annoying!"

Then as I began my day's work and was forced to remember the subject matter I'd be covering in this chapter, another thought occurred to me: *You don't have to be so annoyed.*

There was a way for me to correct my kids' behavior without setting such an edgy tone for the day. There always is. There's always a way to deal with discouragement that doesn't give leverage to discontent.

No matter the depth of discouragement or discontent, God will always give me a way of escape, called gratitude.

Crap Factory

Now the opposite is also true, because no matter how good God is to you, the chatterbox will spin it to make it look like your life is the worst.

I know it's crass, but I think it gets the point across: the chatterbox is a crap factory. No matter what goes in, it comes out crap if you give the chatterbox the opportunity to start interfering and misinterpreting.

For example, I was congratulating someone on a big raise a few years ago. I told him I thought it was incredible.

He brushed off my comments. "Ha! I'll tell you what's incredible," he said. "My new tax bill. Through the roof, bro!"

The guy was a crap factory. God gave him a raise. But instead of receiving it as a blessing and turning it back to praise, he let the chatter of discontentment turn it into crap.

I have one even worse than that. A few years ago in our church, we baptized over two thousand people in just *two weekends*. It was an incredible outpouring of God's Spirit, a watermark event in the life of our church, and one of the most amazing spectacles of God's grace I've ever seen.

I was telling another minister about it, and his response still makes me laugh—and cringe—to this day. "Wow! Two thousand people!" he said with astonishment. "Your water bill must have been *outrageous*!"

He went on to question the veracity of the faith of those who had been baptized. Even though I explained to him how we presented the gospel as clearly as possible and didn't water down (couldn't help it) the message or invitation, he wasn't satisfied.

Crap factory, I say. A miraculous report of how God had moved went in, but crap came out. Even two thousand baptisms weren't a pure enough reason to celebrate. Apparently, it's good enough for the angels in heaven to throw a party in celebration, but this pastor's not interested. There are water bills to worry about and tares that need to be separated from the wheat.

And I have still another example, a more personal one.

One night our youngest child, Abbey, was screaming her head off in those high-pitched, nerve-shattering tones that only a one-year-old can produce. Abbey is a completely healthy, delightful, but incredibly vocal little girl. And I'll admit, I don't do so well demonstrating patience during this stage of child development.

But on this particular night, as I was whining to myself about how Abbey wouldn't stop whining, a series of impressions hit me. I believe they were sent by God's Spirit to gently but firmly correct my attitude.

You prayed for that little girl. I gave her to you. Now you're complaining because she's crying—doing what healthy babies do?

Are you really complaining about a blessing that you asked Me for?

Someone else would love to have a little girl crying in their living room tonight, but they don't. You do—and you need to be thankful, even though it's inconvenient right now.

Crap factory.

I needed to shut it down.

All About the Benefits

Gratitude reinterprets the situations in our lives, beginning with the baseline acknowledgment that *we don't deserve any of what we've been given.* It's all a product of God's grace. The eyesight that allowed you to read that last sentence, the mental abilities that allowed you to comprehend it, the manual dexterity that enabled me to type it—all are products of God's grace. The breaths you took while reading the last paragraph—all of them were borrowed.

When you start with this frame of reference, it's hard to be discontent. But discontentment is empowered by a sense of entitlement. And there is an inverse relationship between gratitude and entitlement.

When entitlement is high, gratitude is low.

When gratitude is high, entitlement is low.

Gratitude begins where our sense of entitlement ends.

I remember the first time I accepted a job with benefits. It felt like winning the Powerball jackpot to hear that, in addition to my salary, my employer would be paying for my health insurance. I had been self-employed until this point and had picked up all those expenses myself.

I was stunned and thankful, and I started proudly telling my friends, "Check it out, check it out. In my new job I've got *benefits.*"

They did not seem impressed. Their responses were "Yeah, that's kind of the way it works, man. It's a part of the package."

They know the system. They had worked jobs with benefits for years. The thrill was gone for them, and it didn't take long for me to lose mine too. Within days something that at first seemed like a tremendous benefit became just a part of the package to me.

I think the same thing happens in our relationship with God.

Most of us can point back to a time in our lives when God's mercy seemed too good to be true. The fact that we could open the Bible and God would speak timeless truth to us in a timely way, specifically to our situation, was a benefit we could never repay. We couldn't get over it.

But then a sense of entitlement sets in. And the things we used to *get* to do—serve God, come to Him in prayer, tell others about what He's done in our lives—become things that we've *got* to do.

Discontentment dies every time you *remember.*

In an earlier chapter we talked about the importance of remembering the price Jesus has paid in order to take our stand against condemnation in the righteousness of Christ. But when thoughts of discontent storm my heart, it's important that I have set up armed guards of remembrance of the Father's blessings in order to keep them at bay.

The attacks of discouragement will never stop coming. But if they're met with praise at the gate, they won't find entrance into my heart.

I believe David wrote the words of this psalm as much to instruct himself as anybody else:

> Praise the LORD, my soul;
>   all my inmost being, praise his holy name.
> Praise the LORD, my soul,
>   and forget not all his benefits—
> who forgives all your sins
>   and heals all your diseases,
> who redeems your life from the pit
>   and crowns you with love and compassion,
> who satisfies your desires with good things
>   so that your youth is renewed like the eagle's. (Psalm 103:1–5)

When it comes to our relationship with God, nothing is of higher importance and greater significance than gratitude. There is no more game-changing resolution than this:

I will not let the discouragement of what I'm going through make me forget the benefits of belonging to the God who has been so good to me. He has saved me, blessed me, forgiven me, restored me, satisfied me, healed me, crowned me, and re-newed me.

When you start thinking, talking, and living like that, God sets up camp in the middle of your situation. And no matter where you look, you see a way you can, because the One who is always with you says you can.

Gratitude is the perspective that looks back and considers God faithful. This enables your faith to look ahead, believing God is able.

Discouragement, condemnation, fear, and insecurity find no base of operation in the heart that is filled with praise and gratitude.

GRATITUDE BEGINS
WHERE OUR SENSE
OF ENTITLEMENT ENDS.

#CRASHTHECHATTERBOX

CONCLUSION

Pound the Ground

All shall be done, but it may be harder than you think.

—C. S. LEWIS, *THE LION, THE WITCH AND THE WARDROBE*

B y now I've told you almost everything I know to tell about crashing the chatterbox. It feels like just the right moment to wrap things up, to do a quick drive-by review of the ground we've covered so far. Perhaps you were expecting me to group the teachings into a list: Seven Power Principles to Crash That Chatterbox. I'm sure there would be value in that. After all, I believe the tools we've discovered from Scripture actually work in real life—if you work them. They certainly have served me well, though—as you're well aware by now—I haven't mastered any of them.

Yet one of the interesting things about the Bible is its almost relentless insistence on defying the easy ending, the neat wrap-up that brings together all the themes and key ideas in perfect symmetry. Even in the biblical narratives of A-list characters we have come to know and love, the stories of their lives often come to jagged ends. The Bible, like real life, resists the simplifications of a thirty-minute sitcom and refuses to tidy up a messy ending just so we can walk away feeling better. (Though, oddly enough, perhaps we end up walking away feeling better to know that these stories are in fact as complex as our own—thus we are not alone.)

So I'd like to leave you with an open-ended closing.

My recent book *Greater* was based on the story of the great biblical prophet Elisha. The Elisha stories are some of the richest and best loved in the Old Testament. In the book I retold some of the best-known Elisha stories and even tried to mine some of the more obscure ones.

But I decided to leave out the story of his final miracle—the one that occurs just before his death. I didn't know quite what to do with it because it felt out of place. For a man who lived such a big life, his final recorded act seemed anti-climactic—such an odd note to end on.

If a director were filming a movie about Elisha's life, I imagine he too would skip this particular scene, especially if he wanted to sell a lot of tickets at the box office.

So I ended the book on a high note, a final suggestive scene after Elisha's death where another man comes back to life simply by making contact with the prophet's brittle bones. It got the job done.

But now, as we come to the end of this book, I want to pick up that old reel off the cutting-room floor.

Despite the epic quality of Elisha's life, his story comes to a close with the world's most remarkable prophet in the unremarkable posture in which so many people ultimately end their lives—sick, presumably in bed, grateful for the life he led, now ready for the tide of death to carry him out.

But as the old man attempts to live his final hours in peace, there is one final disruption. For no matter how precious those final hours should have been, kings have no special regard for such moments. And Israel's leader, King Jehoash, has to contend with the threat of the Arameans.

He rushes to the side of the prophet, who is only hours away from his last breath. But the king is not there to pay his respects, only to make a final request before the light in Elisha's eyes fades. As he stands in the presence of the man of God, the proud, regally dressed king comes unglued. He cries out in anguish, "My father! My father! The chariots and horsemen of Israel!"[1]

What he says in his outburst shows his affection and regard for Elisha, but it also echoes Elisha's own words when *his* spiritual father, Elijah, was taken up to heaven in a chariot.[2] Yet Elisha also understands in Jehoash's words what has brought the panicked king to Elisha's deathbed: *We are under attack. Our chariots are not going to be enough. Our horsemen are under threat. Their army is bigger and better than our army.*

If the years have clouded the ailing prophet's eyes, they have not weakened his spirit. His voice still rumbling with the same bone-chilling authority he'd spoken with in his prime, the prophet gives the king an order. "Take a bow and arrows," Elisha says.

The king does so.

While the king holds the bow and arrow ready in his hands, Elisha calls him to his side. He lays his knotted hands on the king's arm. Here is one last opportunity for the prophet to shape the destinies of the nations. He gives King Jehoash final instructions:

> "Open the east window," he said, and he opened it. "Shoot!" Elisha said, and he shot. "The LORD's arrow of victory, the arrow of victory over Aram!" Elisha declared. "You will completely destroy the Arameans at Aphek."
>
> Then he said, "Take the arrows," and the king took them. Elisha told him, "Strike the ground." He struck it three times and stopped.
> (2 Kings 13:17–18)

So many times in Israel's history, kings ignored the counsel and warnings of prophets. But at last here is a king who listens to the words of the prophet, a great man who does exactly what he was instructed to do. He heeds Elisha's words with precision, striking the ground with the arrows not once, not twice, but three times.

Crash! Crash! Crash!

But then abruptly, before the sound becomes a beat, he stops.

And this is where the quirky little archery lesson descends into the bizarre. Scripture says, "The man of God was angry with him." The storm of his wrath seems to appear out of nowhere. From the cloud of indignation, he berates the king for his actions:

> You should have struck the ground five or six times; then you would have defeated Aram and completely destroyed it. But now you will defeat it only three times. (verse 19)

It is a provocative scene. The king had come to Elisha for help, demonstrating rare humility. Elisha responded by giving him something to do (strike the arrow against the ground). And King Jehoash had obeyed.

Why is this not enough for Elisha? Why the Bobby Knight outburst? And what precisely did the king do wrong?

We are expecting resolution to this cryptic little tale when the story of Elisha's life ends not with a bang but a thud:

Then Elisha died, and they buried him. (verse 20, NKJV)

And that is all. There is no commentary; there is no further insight. Only a matter-of-fact conclusion to a life that was stranger than fiction. During his years of ministry, Elisha had performed twice as many miracles as his predecessor, Elijah.

Then Elisha died.

Then Elisha was buried.

Thank you and good night.

And with that unsatisfying, unsettling ending...

[Fade to black.]

The screen flickers one more time.

So why include Elisha's last recorded miracle here? Because I think buried beneath the rubble of this last Elisha story is the untidy ending we must read if we are going to win the war against the chatterbox, not just a handful of battles.

It comes down to how many times you pound the ground.

In antiquity you rarely won a war with one or two major battles. There were no atomic bombs to drop to take out the enemy with one blast. You were going to have to win a fourth and a fifth and a sixth battle...and probably a seventh and an eighth and beyond. Wars often required near constant waging. Consider the generations of Israelites who were called on to take up arms against the Midianites, Edomites, and Philistines.

Every time King Jehoash pounded the ground with an arrow, it represented another battle Israel would win. Some historical evidence indicates that Jehoash was aware of this dynamic. So when he pounded the ground with the arrow three times, it guaranteed that the people of God would have three decisive military victories over their enemies. This would be enough to weaken the Arame-ans. But it would not be enough to defeat them for good.

Now it's clear why the tired old prophet could not help but use the last of his energy to show his outrage. He was not upset at King Jehoash for lacking faith. If the king didn't believe God could grant him the victory, he wouldn't have come to the prophet of God asking for a miracle. Elisha wasn't upset at the king for being disobedient. The king technically carried out the commands he was given well enough; he did precisely what he was asked to do. What made the veins dance through the leathery skin of the weathered old man's bald head was to see a king who had faith in the living God, and even the humility to do what He asks, settle for something less than *complete victory*.

To see the king stand toe-to-toe with an opportunity to drive out his enemies entirely—but settle for this?

He technically obeyed. He went through the motions, but the king didn't finish. Such astonishing potential, such a halfhearted application.

That's not just sad; that's a tragedy.

Elisha surveys the wreckage of wasted opportunity, and he seethes: "Is that all you've got? Is that all you want? Just enough victory to back the enemy off, just enough to survive? Just enough not to get plundered anymore?

"Why did you stop striking?! If you had kept striking, you would have completely destroyed the enemy! Why would you settle for winning a few battles when you had the opportunity to win the war?"

It would not have taken great intelligence, courage, or ingenuity for the people of God to have defeated their archenemies. All it would have taken was a little more perseverance on the part of the king. He didn't need to learn anything new, beef up the artillery, sharpen the military strategy; he just needed to pound the ground a few more times, and victory was his.

It wasn't a matter of technique. It was a matter of tenacity.

King Jehoash must have known what Elijah—Elisha's spiritual father—had reckoned with in the solitude of the cave: *Every victory you win means another battle you will have to fight.*

Jehoash wasn't lacking in faith or humility. He just stopped pounding the ground for the same pedestrian reason we all stop striking—he got tired of fighting the battles.

####

Here's the bad news:

The chatterbox will not stop talking. It never, ever, ever stops.

The impulses of insecurity never stop poking at your confidence.

The forces of fear never stop pushing against your dreams.

The crow of condemnation never stops sounding off with a *cock-a-doodle-doo*.

The dread of discouragement never stops draining your energy for your assignment.

Chatterboxing is a full-time occupation, because the chatterbox takes no breaks, and it takes no prisoners. The chatterbox is portable. You can go on vacation, but it takes no time off and never takes sick days. The chatterbox is not squeamish with intimate moments. It will go with you to the bathroom or the shower. You can change the scenery, change partners, change your clothes. But the lips of the maniacal chatterbox keep on moving.

You can sabotage it. You can subvert it. But you cannot silence it. The chatterbox always has a few more words to share.

Here's the good news:

When you've defeated the chatterbox once, you have the capacity to beat it every time. The key is persistence.

If you'll keep pounding, victory will keep coming. And even when you lose, you'll gain strength you didn't previously have. When the battle comes around again, you'll be better prepared for it.

####

Through this book God has placed the arrows in your hand—arrows of truth and faith. It will not require your strength or power to win the battles or to win the war. All that will be required of you is trust and tenacity.

Whatever you do, determine to never stop pounding the ground, never stop crashing the box.

I know you are weary. I know you've fought many of these battles before and often lost. But unlike King Jehoash, you can't stop after hitting the ground three times. There is too much at stake, too much hope in you, too much life in you, too much promise in you—too much Christ in you.

Show up for battle—and then show up the next day to fight again. And then show up the next day after that, and then show up the next day after that.

Thought by thought, moment by moment, keep pounding, keep asking and believing, keep crashing.

Believe what God has already declared to be true about you. Resist the lies.

Enjoy the brief reprieve with every victory God grants you, but keep the gloves close by, knowing that if you will simply keep making contact, ultimate victory is yours.

It's just an arrow in the ground, but to God it demonstrates a commitment of the heart: *I refuse to forfeit a victory that God has already given because of a battle that I don't feel like fighting.*

God hasn't brought you this far just to win a few battles. God hasn't brought you this far just to feel a little bit better about managing your life. God didn't save you to just get by, to just exist, to just barely make it through the day. He wants you to experience the total victory of hearing His voice above all others.

Of course, the same old lies will come back and contradict all this—every word of it. The same insecurities, fears, condemnations, discouragements. But when they come back, let 'em know you have a little something for 'em: a promise from God that you've learned how to aim straight for the heart.

There is never anything new about your enemy's tactics or his weapons. It's just the same old lies recycled and reincarnated. Sometimes they seem a little scarier or appear a little more complex.

But defeating them only requires one weapon: the living and active promises of God. Applied personally to your life.

The chatterbox doesn't crash because you underlined some sentences or gleaned some truths. Highlighters and mental assent don't crash or change anything.

But this stuff will work—if you work it.

The chatterbox will crash…

if you pound the ground…

and pound it again…

and again.

Don't stop after three times. You could. Most Christians do. ·

Survival mode. Partial victory.

Endless information but very little transformation.

You could stop there.

Or you can keep pounding.

You can wield the promises of God, sharper than a two-edged sword, and keep accepting, affirming, and believing. Until you see significant patterns of change in the way your heart communes with God and the way you engage your world.

Pound the ground until the pounding becomes a rhythm.

Pound the ground until the sound turns into a cadence.

Pound the ground until the ground starts to shake.

Relentless. Steady. Consistent.

Pound the ground until the erratic *clomp* of your arrow on the floor falls into the slow, steady driving rhythm of a heartbeat.

Pound the ground until it becomes second nature to strike the ground, your new default.

Pound the ground until the shaky clasp of your sweaty palms around the arrow feels normal.

Pound the ground until the soft flesh on your fingers develops more than a few calluses.

Pound the ground until the driving rhythm becomes the backbeat of your life, until it becomes the music you dance to and the war drum you announce battle with.

CRASH!

CRASH!

CRASH!

CRASH!

CRASH!

CRASH!

God says I am. *CRASH!*

God says He will. *CRASH! CRASH!*

God says He has. *CRASH! CRASH! CRASH!*

God says I can. *CRASH! CRASH! CRASH! CRASH!*

Aim. Release. Repeat.

CRASH!

CALLING ALL CHATTERBOXERS

We live in a world full of chatter. Lies of condemnation, fear, insecurity, and discouragement bombard us every day. All the people around you are fighting off their own chatterboxes. Your friends. Your spouse. Your coworkers. The young woman taking your order at Starbucks.

But the battle isn't ours to fight alone.

The good news is, now that you have the tools to fight with, the Enemy doesn't stand a chance. Not only can you crash your own chatterbox, but you can become the catalyst of change for others as they expose the lies they hear inside their own heads.

My team and I have created specific resources to amplify what God is already doing in your life and to equip you to lead the charge against the chatterbox for the people all around you. For example, we want you to be the voice of encouragement for a friend. The leader of a small group designed to build a team of willing world changers. The ambassador in your circles to develop empowering habits that stifle the Enemy.

On your campus. At the office. In your neighborhood.

We are calling all chatterboxers to step up and fight.

Visit crashthechatterbox.com and click on the "Calling All Chatterboxers" link. Here you will find many options for how to take what you've learned through this book, decide what works best for you, and spread the word, prompting others to experience liberation from the chatterbox.

So lace up the gloves. And join the thousands of other chatterboxers already in the middle of the action.

DISCUSSION QUESTIONS

Section 1: God Says I Am
Overpowering lies of insecurity

Please read the introduction and chapters 1–4 of *Crash the Chatterbox*.

Recap: The voices of our chatterboxes are the lies resounding inside our minds that keep us from hearing the voice of God. One major way the chatterbox lies is by telling us that God could never want some-one like us. But if we are following Christ, then God wants us to know that He *does* love and ac-cept us. And this acceptance isn't grudging, as if God *has* to accept us because it's a part of the deal worked out on the cross. Rather, He genuinely *likes* us. The Enemy will undoubtedly raise ques-tions and inspire doubts about what God has said about us, but we can reverse these attacks by af-firming the truths of God about who we are.

> **The chatterbox says**
> *I am worthless and rejected.*
>
> **God says**
> *I am His beloved child through Christ.*

1. What are the main messages your chatterbox has been bombarding you with lately?
2. How have you noticed the lies from your chatterbox drowning out the words of truth from God? Can you give an example or two?
3. In what ways do you suffer from insecurity in your relationship with God?
4. Read Ephesians 1:3–14. Keeping in mind that *identity* trumps *insecurity*, what does this passage teach you about who you are in Christ?
5. Pastor Steven says,

   [God] has not chosen you blindly but intentionally, even while knowing you inwardly and intimately. And let me tell you why

this is some of the best news in the history of the universe: if
this God has chosen you while totally knowing even the worst
parts of you, then you no longer have to live *up* to anything.
Instead, you are now empowered to live *out* of an awareness of
divine acceptance.

How does the reality of your acceptance by God free you to live
differently?

6. Have you ever felt in your heart, *God may love me, but I wonder if He
   really likes me*? If so, what was the context for that chatterbox lie? What
   did it do to you?

7. What evidence do you have that God's favor rests upon you?

8. How has the Enemy tried to twist or cast doubt on affirming things you
   know God has said about you? (For examples of some of the affirming
   things God says, see chapter 2.)

9. What truths from Scripture can you think of to contradict the lies of
   insecurity you've been hearing from your chatterbox?

10. What do you think God wants to say to you right now about who you are
    in His eyes and how He feels about you?

Section 2: God Says He Will
Overpowering lies of fear

Read chapters 5–7.

Recap: The second major area where the chatterbox lies is by convincing us
that we should be scared about what could happen to us in this life. But God
commands us to kick fear out of our lives. We do this through the counteractive force of faith—we choose to trust in God's love and care for us. One
strategy that helps is to mentally complete our fearful scenario using the sentence starters "What if…?" (for example, What if the car repair bill is more
than I can afford?), "That would…" (That would be inconvenient), and "God
will…" (God will help me figure something out). Then, trusting that God is
greater than our fears, we need to act in faithfulness to Him. In communica-

tion theory terms, we need to tune out the noise of fear so that we can tune in to the signal of God's reassuring words to us. And follow Him.

1. What are your worst or most frequently recurring fears?

2. How do these fears hinder you from living the way you think God wants you to live?

3. Consider this statement: *Faith, not courage, is the opposite of fear.* Do you agree or disagree, and why?

4. Read Psalm 23. What do you think gave David his spirit of confidence? Would you say you share that spirit of confidence? Why or why not?

> **The chatterbox says** the future is full of danger.
>
> **God says** He will preserve and protect me.

5. Pick one of the biggest fears in your life right now, and play it out to its logical conclusion (*God's* logic, remember, not the *Enemy's!*) by completing these sentences:

   What if _____?

   That would _____.

   God will _____.

6. How does this exercise change your perspective on this area of fear?

7. In what ways is God calling you to push through your fears by acting in faithfulness to Him? What might you achieve if you do it? What might you miss out on if you disobey?

8. How is the noise of your fear interfering with the signal of God's reassuring words to you? Give an example.

9. What specific scriptures could you read, meditate on, and memorize to help counteract the fears you are feeling?

10. What do you think God wants to say to you right now about your future?

Section 3: God Says He Has
Overpowering lies of condemnation

Read chapters 8–10.

Recap: Another area where the chatterbox is frequently active is condemnation. When you do something wrong, the Enemy tries to make you feel worse about yourself than you should feel. Of course it's good

> **The chatterbox says**
> my mistakes
> disqualify me from
> God's love.
>
> **God says**
> I am His beloved
> child through Christ.

to make a realistic assessment of a sin and to repent of it—but that's totally different from thinking you're worthless and have forfeited God's love. The Enemy's *condemnation* of your very being is completely distinct from the Holy Spirit's *conviction* of your sin. You can recognize condemnation because it encourages you to evaluate your error as personal (*What's wrong with me?*), permanent (*I always...*), and pervasive (...*mess up everything!*).

The truth is, God says He has forgiven you—and He has. To triumph over condemnation, you need to keep in mind the Lord's gracious acceptance of you in Christ and quit dwelling on your failures.

1. Think of a time when you messed up big time. What messages about yourself did you hear in your head afterward?
2. How has a sense of condemnation affected you (such as in your choices, your ministry, or your relationships with Christ and other people)?
3. Pastor Steven says,

> The Enemy wants to magnify our failures to the millionth power with his exaggerations so he can pervert the power of the Spirit's conviction. Ignoring the Enemy's accusations is impossible. Besides, we don't want to minimize the nature or ramifications of sin. But we must develop the habit of separating our sense of worth from our appraisal of our behavior. It's the only way we can rightly deal with our sin practically, confident in the fact that God has already *dealt* with it—eternally.

If you were to come up with a list of dos and don'ts about dealing with your errors, what would the list include?

4. How do you recognize the Holy Spirit's conviction of sin when it comes?

5. How is the outcome of conviction different from the outcome of condemnation?

6. Describe a time when your chatterbox used one, two, or all three of the *p*'s of condemnation.

> *Personal*—The chatterbox says your sin shows what a fundamentally bad person you are.

> *Permanent*—The chatterbox says the sin illustrates how you *always* mess up.

> *Pervasive*—The chatterbox says this one sin shows what a screwup you are in all sorts of areas.

7. When the chatterbox starts spewing condemnation, what's something you could do to help yourself *remember* God's forgiveness?

8. What's something you could do to help yourself *forget* your failures?

9. The biblical chapter that begins, "There is now no condemnation for those who are in Christ Jesus," ends with a stirring statement about the inability of condemnation to drive a wedge between Christ and us (Romans 8:31–39). After reading this passage, how do you think you can react better when the voices of condemnation start to chatter in your head?

10. What do you think God wants to say to you right now about your position with Him?

Section 4: God Says I Can
Overpowering lies of discouragement

Read chapters 11–13 and conclusion.

Recap: The last weapon of the chatterbox is discouragement. All of Jesus's followers, whether famous or obscure, are vulnerable to downer thoughts about their lives and their relationship with Christ. Such temptation to be discouraged is not something we can realistically hope to get past. But we can defy the inertia of discouragement. You see, when the Enemy tries to discourage us, he's hoping we'll stop trusting in God's plan. So we should realize that facing doubts and discouragement can actually be confirmation that we are being obedient in our calling. (Because otherwise, why would the Enemy be trying to detour us?) When there's a gap between our expectations and reality, we have to trust that God is still working out His plans.

> **The chatterbox says**
> I can't be the person or accomplish the things I want.
>
> **God says**
> I can do all things through Christ who strengthens me.

One key to persevering while we wait for God is to remember all the wonderful things that God has done and is still doing for us—and be grateful.

1. What have you been discouraged about lately?

2. Pastor Steven says,

   Going to the next level isn't about graduating from difficult circumstances and dark emotions. It's resolving to live with the mind-set that declares, *My joy is not determined by what happens to me but by what Christ is doing in me and through me.*

   How do your own experiences help to confirm that conclusion?

3. Read 2 Corinthians 12:1–10. How does Paul's experience serve as a paradigm for us in facing tough circumstances despite spiritual advancement? In learning about perseverance through disappointment?

4. Who are some mature believers you know who have dealt with discouraging situations? What have you learned from their reaction?

5. What do you think *the Enemy* is trying to accomplish through current situations in your life that aren't what you expected or wanted? What do you think *God* is trying to accomplish through them?

6. What gives you hope amid your discouragement?

7. What are some of the greatest blessings in your life that you can thank God for?

8. If you wanted to make gratitude to God an enduring quality of your life, how would you go about it? How might it change you?

9. What do you think God wants to say to you right now about what you can be and what you can accomplish?

10. What are the areas in your life where you think you're going to have to be unrelenting from now on in crashing the chatterbox?

NOTES

Chapter 1: Subverting the Sabotage

1. John 8:44.
2. Romans 7:22–23.
3. Brennan Manning, *Abba's Child: The Cry of the Heart for Intimate Belonging* (Colorado Springs: NavPress, 1994), 107.
4. Steven Pressfield, *The War of Art: Break Through the Blocks and Win Your Inner Creative Battles* (New York: Grand Central Publishing, 2002), 42.
5. Genesis 1:3.
6. Thomas Watson, quoted in R. Bruce Bickel, *Light and Heat: The Puritan View of the Pulpit* (Morgan, PA: Soli Deo Gloria, 1999), 12.
7. Isaiah 55:3, NKJV.
8. 2 Corinthians 10:5.
9. 2 Corinthians 10:4.

Chapter 2: Cancel the Audition

1. Galatians 4:5–7.
2. I am His masterpiece (Ephesians 2:10, NLT); I am His workmanship (Ephesians 2:10, NKJV); I am established (2 Corinthians 1:21, NKJV); I am sealed with His promise (John 6:27, NKJV); I am redeemed (Colossians 1:14; NIV).
3. Matthew 5:14, emphasis added.
4. I am loved (John 15:9); I am more than a conqueror (Romans 8:35–37); I am strong and courageous (Deuteronomy 31:6); I am healed and whole (1 Peter 2:24); I am forgiven and free (1 John 1:9).

Chapter 3: God Likes Me Too

1. Hebrews 12:6.

Chapter 4: Who Told You That?

1. Genesis 3:9.

2. Genesis 3:10.

3. Genesis 3:11.

4. See Matthew 4:3, 6, 9.

5. Matthew 4:4, 7, 10.

6. See Romans 5:14.

7. Matthew 27:22–23.

8. Isaiah 53:7.

9. Romans 8:15 (NIV, 1984).

10. Romans 8:16.

Chapter 5: So What If...

1. Joseph Heller, *Something Happened* (New York: Dell, 1966), 3.

2. Matthew 4:39.

Chapter 6: At the Bottom

1. Colossians 3:1.

2. 1 Peter 2:6; Psalm 32:7; Psalm 3:3; Psalm 51:12; Philippians 4:7; Psalm 71:20; Isaiah 42:7; Psalm 41:11; James 1:2–5; Psalm 37:23–24; Hebrews 4:16; 1 Kings 8:28; Ezekiel 37:9; Psalm 91:4; James 4:7–8; Hebrews 1:14.

3. Susan Jeffers, *Feel the Fear...and Do It Anyway* (New York: Fawcett Columbine, 1987), 57, 59.

4. Jeffers, *Feel the Fear,* 59.

5. Jeffers, *Feel the Fear,* 28.

6. Matthew 25:21, 23.

7. John 15:15.

8. See 2 Timothy 1:7, NKJV.

Chapter 7: What Are You Doing Here?

1. Matthew 4:4; Deuteronomy 8:3.

2. Jon Gertner, "Most Creative People 2013, No. 1 Nate Silver," *Fast Company,* June 2013, www.fastcompany.com/3009258/most-creative-people -2013/1-nate-silver.

3. New International Version.

4. New King James Version.

5. Psalm 46:1; 139:16.
6. 1 John 4:4.

Chapter 8: Finishing the Devil's Sermons

1. Revelation 12:10.
2. Arthur W. Pink, *A. W. Pink's Studies in the Scriptures, 1936–1937a,* vol. 8, comp. Jay P. Green Jr. (Mulberry, IN: Sovereign Grace Publishers, 2003), 376.
3. *Fiddler on the Roof,* directed by Norman Jewison (1971; Los Angeles: MGM, 2007), DVD.

Chapter 9: Counterfeit Conviction

1. Jerry Bridges, *The Pursuit of Holiness* (Colorado Springs: NavPress, 2006), 48.
2. Henry Cloud, *Boundaries for Leaders: Results, Relationships, and Being Ridiculously in Charge* (New York: HarperBusiness, 2013), 110.
3. Cloud, *Boundaries for Leaders,* 112.
4. Matthew 7:3–5.
5. Lysa TerKeurst, *Unglued: Making Wise Choices in the Midst of Raw Emotions* (Grand Rapids, MI: Zondervan, 2012), 32–33.
6. Oswald Chambers, *My Utmost for His Highest* (Uhrichsville, OH: Barbour, 1963), April 19.

Chapter 10: The Divine Reminder

1. Donald Miller, *A Million Miles in a Thousand Years: What I Learned While Editing My Life* (Nashville: Thomas Nelson, 2009), 3, emphasis added.
2. See Matthew 26:33, 35.
3. Matthew 16:18.
4. George Santayana, *The Life of Reason, or, The Phases of Human Progress* (New York: Scribner's, 1906), 284.

Chapter 11: Keep Rolling

1. Mother Teresa, *Mother Teresa: Come Be My Light: The Private Writings of the "Saint of Calcutta,"* ed. Brian Kolodiejchuk (New York: Image, 2009), 192–94.

2. Mother Teresa, *Come Be My Light,* 210.

3. 2 Corinthians 4:8–9.

Chapter 12: The Expectation Gap

1. Matthew 3:12.

2. John 1:29.

3. Rainer Maria Rilke, *Letters to a Young Poet,* trans. Stephen Mitchell (New York: Vintage, 1984), 34.

4. Matthew 14:10–12.

5. Emily Perl Kingsley, "Welcome to Holland." Copyright © 1987. All rights reserved. Reprinted by permission of the author.

Chapter 13: The Parable of the Passport

1. Steven Furtick, *Sun Stand Still: What Happens When You Dare to Ask God for the Impossible* (Colorado Springs: Multnomah, 2010), chap. 7.

Conclusion: Pound the Ground

1. 2 Kings 13:14.

2. 2 Kings 2:12.

ACKNOWLEDGMENTS

I'll resist the temptation to list all the friends, pastors, Elevators, and family members who made me who I am and stood by me through everything, generally speaking. You didn't come to hear an acceptance speech, I know. So, instead, I'll name just a few precious people who were directly instrumental in bringing this book to life. Your ministry is on every page, and your impact is in every heart that is blessed.

Hondale / Killer B. / GTM / Abbey (nickname still in development)—For the inspiration and the interruptions. All things work together, and it's all good.

Faith Bracy—Good life.

Jess M. / Amy C. / Larry H. / Wade J. / Ryan H. / Lysa T.—Subzero owes thanks to no one. But your contribution makes you the exception. Thank you. (So much.)

Chuck Barrett—Thanks for the great title, sub, and chapter ideas. All that was left to do was print 'em!

Steve C.—For Workin' It Out.

Carie F. / Allison / and team—Thanks for pushing!

Dave K.—DAD!

Eric S.—Master of the em dash.

Jonathan M.—Thank God the probation officer gave us a day for the finishing touches. It was a close call.

Bishop Craig G.—If you'd never called and asked, "Hey, how's your book going?" who knows… Thanks for believing in me.

Esther F.—Right?!

Chad B.—Savant.

ABOUT THE AUTHOR

STEVEN FURTICK is the *New York Times* best-selling author of *Greater* and *Sun Stand Still*. He is also the founder and lead pastor of Elevation Church, which since its founding in 2006 has grown to more than thirteen thousand attendees at nine locations. He has spoken at major conferences around the world. He holds a master of divinity degree from Southern Baptist Theological Seminary. He and his wife, Holly, have three young children.

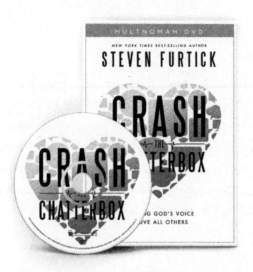

DREAM **BIGGER.** START **SMALLER.**

If you sense that you were meant for more but feel stuck where you are, *Greater* will give you the *confidence* to know that nothing is impossible with God, the *clarity* to see the next step He's calling you to take, and the *courage* to do anything He tells you to do.

>>>

RESOURCES: BOOK | DVD | PARTICIPANT'S GUIDE

IF THE SIZE OF YOUR VISION FOR YOUR LIFE ISN'T INTIMIDATING TO YOU, THERE'S A GOOD CHANCE IT IS INSULTING TO GOD.

In his first book, Pastor Steven Furtick challenges you to walk in audacious faith and watch God do the impossible in your life. No dream is too big when God is involved, and there is unlimited potential in the life of every believer through Jesus. Steven shows that faith is the most vital building block in your relationship with God as you live out what He has put in your heart.

The Sun Stand Still Devotional is a daily personal guide into Scripture as you begin to live the life God created you for.

**FIND OUT MORE ABOUT THE MOVEMENT AT
WWW.SUNSTANDSTILL.ORG**